The Politics of
Kim Campbell

The Politics of Kim Campbell

From School Trustee to Prime Minister

Murray Dobbin

Ellen Gould, Research Associate

James Lorimer & Company, Publishers
Toronto, 1993

James Lorimer & Company Ltd. acknowledges with thanks the support of the Canada Council, the Ontario Arts Council and the Ontario Publishing Centre in the development of writing and publishing in Canada.

Cover photo: © *Vancouver Sun,* Jeff Vinnick

Canadian Cataloguing in Publication Data

Dobbin, Murray, 1945–

   The politics of Kim Campbell : from school trustee to

prime minister.

ISBN 1-55028-431-2 (bound) ISBN 1-55028-413-4 (pbk.)

1. Campbell, Kim, 1947–   . 2. Cabinet ministers - Canada -
Biography.* 3. Politicians - Canada - Biography.
I. Title.

FC631.C3D6 1993 971.064'7'092 C93-094451-8
F1034.3.C3D6 1993

James Lorimer & Company Ltd., Publishers
Egerton Ryerson Memorial Building
35 Britain Street
Toronto, Ontario M5A 1R7

Printed and bound in Canada

Contents

Acknowledgements

My partner, Ellen Gould, made the book possible with her knowledge of defence issues, her contributions to the analysis of the Campbell phenomenon, her editing and research, and her translation of French media coverage of Kim Campbell — not to mention her patience with an author in full-fledged book-writing mode.

My editor, Diane Young, went far beyond the call of duty to meet deadlines only the slightly crazed would dare to impose. I am also grateful to Cy Strom for his careful copy edit of the manuscript and to Melinda Tate who input the editorial changes and helped fact check.

Allan Engler helped with research on Campbell's history in British Columbia politics. Heather Wardle searched through newspapers for relevant articles. Many journalists gave generously of their time and analysis in conversations over the course of the writing of the book. Several dozen people agreed to be interviewed about Campbell's politics. Kim Campbell, however, was not one of them, despite repeated requests. Allan Garr's excellent book on Bill Bennett, *Tough Guy,* was invaluable in understanding Kim Campbell and what we might expect from a Campbell government. Kate Abbott at the Pacific Press library was very helpful in providing photo resources on Kim Campbell's political career.

The flaws in the book are, of course, my own.

I would like to acknowledge a grant from the Ontario Arts Council's fund for out-of-province writers.

Introduction

Brian Mulroney is gone after nine long years that many Canadians would like to forget. The Canadian political scene and the country's social and economic direction have undergone such wrenching changes during the Mulroney years that it is hard to predict the long-term consequences for our political culture or our country. Social programs once described as "sacred trusts" are being either eliminated or cut back. National institutions such as the CBC, the Canada Council, and VIA Rail are now at risk. Massive changes in the country's economic base have been precipitated by free trade; these changes have left half a million people out of work. The government's focus on fighting inflation has maintained high levels of unemployment that are unprecedented for the post–World War II era, and tax breaks to the wealthy and corporations have resulted in crushing levels of taxation for the middle class and escalating levels of public debt. All of these experiences have battered and bruised the average Canadian.

Into the political vacuum comes Kim Campbell, promising change and a fresh approach. Campbell has been able to capitalize on the same culture of discontent that gave a platform for Preston Manning and his Reform Party. Liberal leader Jean Chrétien and NDP leader Audrey McLaughlin, despite their opposition to most of Mulroney's policies, still represent the old guard to many Canadians. There is a yearning for someone — something — new.

Campbell packaged herself as the "new and fresh face," the "new direction," the candidate of "inclusive politics" who will consult with us before imposing measures like the GST. It is an image that Canadians want to believe. And there is a part of Kim Campbell that fits that image.

One enduring image of Campbell is the one she presented when giving her explanation of the "naked shoulders" photograph. Asked to respond to the sudden media interest in the photo, she replied as you might want her to reply — with humour and genuine candour. She said that she thought it was "a hoot." After listening to the unctuous baritone of Mulroney or the tired political posturing of his other cabinet members, it was a refreshing change. Defying all the odds for someone on the Mulroney team, there seemed to be a real human being here, someone who did not take herself too seriously, who was not always puffed up with self-importance. Someone who was not a man, did not behave like man, but who had managed to make it in a world of ambitious and self-important men.

The extent to which people wanted to believe that image was only made clear when Brian Mulroney finally announced that he was quitting. The first reaction to the announcement was celebrated on CBC's "Friday Night with Ralph Benmergui" by the entire audience joining Ralph in a chorus of "He's gone, he's gone." It was a cathartic moment. What shocked many people, though, were the polls that said how well a renewed Conservative Party would do in an election, specifically with *Kim Campbell* as the new Tory leader. She would, said one of the first polls, win 43 percent of the vote compared to 25 percent for Jean Chrétien.

Could people's memories really be that short? Was hatred of Brian Mulroney as an individual so intense and were hopes for the post-Mulroney Canada so great, that people would actually give the Conservative Party another term in office? Analysts scurried about, trying to figure out what it all meant. Part of the answer was that opponents of the Tories could never resist attacking Mulroney rather than his government. No prime minister had ever presented such an inviting target. He took the blame for nearly all of the anger at what his government had done. And now it seemed he would take much of it with him when he left.

Both the Tory party and the media did their best, in the weeks that followed, to fix this attitude in the minds of the Canadian public. If it had not been for Campbell overplaying "inclusiveness" and for her many gaffes and misstatements, Campbellmania might still be with us. And among delegates to the Conservative Party leadership convention, it turned out that Campbell's gaffes and arrogance did not matter — her campaign organizers and spin doctors could get her elected in spite of herself. What that revealed, among other things, was that the majority of delegates apparently thought that they could win the next federal election no matter who their leader was. That should concern all Canadians who yearn for their country to take a different direction, to make a real change from the Mulroney program.

The Conservative Party wants to be re-elected in order to complete the work that Brian Mulroney began. Campbell wants to complete Brian Mulroney's transformation of Canada. When Campbell appeared before her volunteers after her victory, they started chanting "Four more years!" Campbell shook her head and yelled "Ten more years!" — reminiscent of Margaret Thatcher when she promised that she would take the British Conservative Party into the next millennium.

Canadians' yearning for change at any cost could backfire if it keeps them from using their good judgement. That same yearning took Preston Manning and his party to 16 percent in the polls, until people began to examine more closely what he was saying and what it meant. We need to do the same with any leader. Campbell is no exception.

It can be difficult to figure out a political leader on the basis of campaign speeches alone. For example, Campbell, like Jean Chrétien and Audrey McLaughlin, talks about creating jobs. Canadians have to dig deeper to find out that when Campbell talks about creating jobs, she would try to do this exactly as Mulroney tried, by cutting taxes and regulations on corporations.

It comes down to this: You cannot know where politicians are going if you do not know where they are coming from. When Campbell leads the Tories into the next election, she will be applying for the job of prime minister and the power to set the country's course for the future. We need to examine her résumé.

Campbell advances as part of her credentials that she was in Mulroney's inner cabinet. What role did she play there? Did she try to moderate the Tory agenda or did she promote it aggressively? Campbell's experience as Justice Minister is the basis of her claim to represent a new kind of politics. What specifically did she do to justify this claim? Did the people who dealt with Campbell in her riding and in her successive ministerial portfolios — Indian Affairs, Justice and Defence — feel that they were being welcomed to engage in a new style of politics?

Also on Campbell's résumé is her experience as a member of the Social Credit government of Bill Bennett in British Columbia, where she was very close to the centre of power. Bennett's government led the way in Canada in introducing Draconian cutbacks to social programs. He also pioneered what has been called the "big bang" approach — concealing the agenda of cuts and privatization during an election and then implementing it in one massive assault early on so that opposition forces would be overwhelmed. By the time the next election came, so much time had elapsed that the changes seemed irreversible. Did Campbell go along with this strategy? Would she be likely to implement it if she wins the next election?

We also need to know how Campbell behaved when she was on the Vancouver school board, because that level of government is the closest of all to the day-to-day needs of ordinary citizens. Here again we can gauge her claim to a new kind of politics — "inclusive" politics, as Campbell calls it.

We need to take Campbell seriously when she says that she is an intellectually driven politician. She has said repeatedly that her favourite political philosopher is Edmund Burke. We must discover exactly what that means. What did Edmund Burke stand for? What did he have to say about how democracy should function? Finally, we need to know who Campbell's closest associates and advisors are. Who is at her side as she exercises her power as prime minister? What kind of people helped her become elected leader of the Conservative Party, and what sorts of favours will they be expecting in return? And what does her choice of advisors and associates say about her promise of change and consultation?

We cannot effectively assess whether we want Kim Campbell to run the country for the next five years without knowing her record, her political philosophy, how she has treated ordinary Canadians trying to be heard by government, who her friends and advisors are and what they stand for. But knowing this is not enough.

Canadians must apply their critical intelligence to the political process itself. We are well past the age when politicians used polls simply to find out what we think. There are people working for political parties in this new age of high-tech politics who boast that they can use polls, focus groups, image making and other techniques to make us support things we fundamentally do not believe in. Widespread cynicism about the political process is the inevitable product of this manipulation of politics. Can a political system suffering from years of cynicism and public relations manipulation actually deliver what the majority wants? The result of the 1992 constitutional referendum can offer some hope, regardless of how we feel about the actual contents of the proposal. All the expensive public relations tools that were brought to bear on the Canadian public did not produce a victory for the government. That is why many observers are hopeful that the next federal election will be decided not by the image-makers, but by the informed judgement of the Canadian people who will be affected by its outcome, for better or for worse.

This is a voter's guide to Canada's new prime minister. It is not enough to know that Kim Campbell sometimes puts her foot in her mouth and plays the cello and is willing to be photographed bare-shouldered. It is not enough that she has a sense of humour. And it is not enough that she is a woman who describes herself as a feminist. It is critical that Canadians know what Prime Minister Campbell will do with the power we might hand over to her. I have tried to write a book which helps Canadians answer that question.

The Socred Years

Canadians know a lot about Kim Campbell's early years because of the many feature articles that have appeared since her rapid rise to prominence. Who, by now, does not know that at the age of twelve she changed her name from Avril Phaedra to Kim? Who does not know that her mother, Lissa Vroom, facing the bleak prospect of a bad marriage with an overbearing husband, decided that her only option was to leave her husband and children behind? Lissa Vroom and her new partner, Bill Vroom, worked hard on the yachts of the rich and famous in the Mediterranean and West Indies. As Judy Steed of *The Toronto Star* reported, "She'd been driven into exile, she said, by a bad marriage, having been crippled in a freak accident, in an era when women had no rights to division of matrimonial property."[1] Campbell's mother had spent eight years putting her husband through law school. "He ended up a lawyer and she ended up with no skills to earn a decent living."[2]

Lissa Vroom kept in regular touch with her two children, Kim and her older sister Alix, now a lawyer in Vancouver, specializing in developing computer programs for other lawyers. According to Vroom, "When I was in the West Indies, Kim sent me the family bible — it was one of those pretty white bibles with a zipper round it; my mother gave it to her — and asked me to fill in the family tree."[3]

When Campbell says she was brought up to be a feminist, the statement likely reflects her mother's independent life and intellectual influence. "I suppose it would be hard for anyone raised on the sayings of Charlotte Whitton and the poetry of Edna St. Vincent Millay not to turn out a feminist." Lissa Vroom says she "raised the girls to believe they could do anything they wanted to do."[4]

Lissa Vroom was a woman ahead of her time, says Steed. In one of the few interviews Vroom has permitted, she spoke with erudition and insight of literature, history, and her love of her daughters. "Bernard Shaw said that the only independence worth having was economic independence and I agree with him. He's one of my heroes."[5] She clearly had an impact on her daughter despite being thousands of miles away.

Campbell's father, George, is now retired and was for many years a Vancouver prosecutor. He happily takes credit for the abilities of the daughter who is now so famous. Soon after their mother left, George Campbell took the girls out of the boarding school Lissa had placed them in and brought them home to live with him and his new partner, a woman half his age and not much older than his daughters. The girls did not like the idea of living with their stepmother and remained estranged from their father for many years.

Campbell's immediate family is secretive about her. Lissa Vroom has agreed to be interviewed, but Campbell's sister and two former husbands have declined. According to *Maclean's*, "In an unusual step, [Campbell] has compiled lists of friends, from childhood to the present, who willingly recite harmless anecdotes about her life to reporters."[6]

Campbell apparently took her mother's lessons to heart early on. She was outgoing at school and in her one year at St. Ann's Academy, a Catholic boarding school, amazed her teachers by obtaining a perfect score on an intelligence test.[7] She was the best student they had in thirty-nine years. She considered the year at the academy to be an adventure and rarely talked of the trauma of her parents' separation.

Her adolescence was a "very unhappy" period, according to Campbell, but that was news to those who went to school with her. They recall her as being outgoing and cheerful. That suggests that she put a lot of energy into the aspects of her life over which she could have some control — music, reading and student politics. She was president of her high school student council in 1964 — the first female to win the post — and class valedictorian.

Campbell has always been a Conservative, or so she claims. "I always knew that I was a Conservative — though I didn't really know why until later — in the sense of belonging to a political party. Most of the young people I knew who were the movers and shakers on campus were Liberals, because that was the party in government, and it seemed to me that their main interest was in furthering their careers ... It was like belonging to a nice club and that didn't appeal to me at all."[8]

The influences on Campbell have been written about extensively. Her favourite political philosopher is the eighteenth-century conservative Edmund Burke. His attraction to tradition, stability and social cohesion, his disdain for and fear of social change, and his belief that an intellectual aristocracy should run the affairs of state immediately appealed to Campbell. Perhaps it was the chronic instability of her early life that attracted her to the quintessential voice of stability among political philosophers.

But perhaps the main political influences in her early student life were two powerful men, the one whom she married and the one who immersed her in the politics of anti-communism. The first was Nathan Divinsky, a flamboyant and outspoken professor of mathematics at the University of British Columbia where Campbell was taking her degree in political science. Divinsky — whose nickname was Tuzie — was a renowned chess player who loved to entertain in a grand manner. Even his friends describe him as outrageously right-wing,[9] and he delighted in defending Britain's rigid class system and flaunting his political views.[10] One friend, Fritz Bowers, says of Divinsky, "Tuzie's very reactionary and élitist. He thinks the important thing is to look after the interests of the intelligentsia, the people who lead society."[11] According to Campbell's sister, speaking in 1991, "Nathan had a lot to teach her, and she was hungry to learn."[12]

Campbell points out that the relationship was not a one-way street. "I had as powerful an influence on him as he did on me. There were lots of things I learned in the course of that relationship but the same was true in reverse." [13]

Campbell started dating Divinsky, who is often described as displaying avuncular charm, in 1967. He introduced her to a life of dinner parties and the politics of upper–middle class Vancouver society at a time when the campus she was studying on was in the throes of left-wing student movements and anti–Viet Nam war demonstrations. She was oddly out of place in that era of pot, free love, long hair and Marxism. Stan Persky, the Vancouver author and columnist, was on the student council with her. "She looked like a straight right-winger, well-dressed with fluffy blond hair. I thought, 'Oh, God. Here's the ancient regime.' "[14]

Her own thoughts on the radical politics that were swirling around her are not extensive. She has claimed that she shared some of the concerns of the left-wing students but "could not accept their left-wing dogma." But the way she *did* politics in those early student days was revealing of how she would eventually pursue her career. Don Munton, a fellow student council member and now a professor at the University of British Columbia, recalls, "Some people on the executive would get ticked off because she would go her own way; they thought she broke ranks and grandstanded, but I thought she had a natural instinct for politics. She had an extremely good sense of when to take a stand on a popular issue."[15] It's a telling comment. He did not say that she pushed for issues that she cared about. Her instinct for politics was, as the comment seems to suggest, opportunistic. And her early tendency to grandstand would continue.

Campbell completed her honours degree in political science, but it was the last thing she would complete in her academic career. She started a master's program at UBC and failed to complete it before going on to the London School of Economics to pursue a PhD, which she also failed to finish. This apparent restlessness or lack of perseverance would continue until she found her real calling: politics.

At the London School of Economics, for which she received a four-year Canada Council fellowship, she met the other academic who would influence her politics. That man was Leonard Schapiro, a right-winger who is one of the world's leading authorities on the Soviet Union. He was one of the key figures at the London School of Economics during the sixties and seventies. The school had a reputation as a radical university, but it was the students who were radical at the time. The maintenance of the school's left-wing tradition was in the hands of a few scholars like Ralph Miliband.

Leo Panitch, who teaches political science at York University, was at the London School of Economics just before Campbell arrived. "What's interesting is that she would come to LSE to study under Schapiro. That really demonstrates that she was totally out of synch with her generation. Almost everybody came to study under the left-wing profs. The university was occupied twice in that period by the student left and at one point Schapiro and the others in charge closed the university down for a few months — just locked us out."[16]

Schapiro led Campbell and some other students on a three-month study trip to the Soviet Union. She came back even more contemptuous of left-wing ideology, describing the USSR as "a profligate waste of human potential." If Divinsky had influenced her in a general way towards conservative thinking, Schapiro, and her trip to Russia, put meat on the bones. "Leonard was clear on what mattered. It was from him that I absorbed the idea that the rule of law is the foundation of a free and democratic society."[17]

Campbell's contempt for communism and indeed any collective solution to social problems has been evident from her earliest university days. Reinforced by Divinsky and given substance by Schapiro, it has not changed a shade since. Charlotte Gray wrote of her 1990 conversation with Campbell, " 'To me,' the Justice Minister explained, hands clenched together, 'the ideal society is one where people have the very best opportunity to develop themselves and let their creativity run ... [No] planner can engineer a society [without] diminishing people's self-reliance.' "[18]

There is a good deal of pretension in Campbell's claim to be an intellectual. Campbell is often compared to Trudeau: the aloof intellectual with disdain for the common people. The disdain is there, but as many observers have pointed out, the claim to an intellectual status comparable to Trudeau's is simply false. Campbell has neither published anything as a political thinker nor presented papers at academic conferences. Her repetitions of her Burkean political beliefs hardly compare to Trudeau who was a recognized intellectual force for years in Quebec, writing extensively in *Cité Libre,* developing a vision of his province and the country based on his political philosophy, before becoming involved in electoral politics.

Campbell returned to Canada in 1973 together with Divinsky, who had spent a year's sabbatical with her in Britain. By this point, Campbell and Divinsky were married. After another year with Divinsky in Oregon, Campbell tried her hand at teaching. From 1975 until 1978, she taught at the University of British Columbia, but could not get tenure. She then taught for several years at the community college level. At the end of seven years of teaching, most of it as a sessional lecturer, the bottom of the teaching ladder, Campbell realized that she had hit a dead end. Although she felt that her inability to attract a full-time, tenure-track job was due to sexism, she was probably fortunate to teach at all at the university level with no more than a BA.

If her career to this point was marked by confusion over her goals — "as a result of my genes I have so many choices" — she seemed to finally get it right in her decision to go into law. "I knew

I wanted to go into politics, where the law is a good background, because you can always go back to it."[19]

Joining the Socred Farm Team

In 1980, the same year that she entered law school, Campbell began her political career by successfully running for a seat as trustee on the Vancouver school board. Divinsky had resigned his seat to run for city council and it appeared that Campbell was simply taking her husband's place. Certainly her politics were virtually identical. It was as if she had taken one lesson from Divinsky to heart — the one about how important it is to ensure that the interests of the intelligentsia are looked after. She quickly developed a reputation for a single-minded attachment to one educational issue: more funds and programs for so-called gifted students.

Civic politics in Vancouver is characterized by the same polarization as provincial politics, although the lines are not as clearly partisan. The Committee of Progressive Electors (COPE) has been running left-wing candidates for years, some of whom are also NDPers; the right has responded with its own euphemistically named Non Partisan Association (NPA), made up primarily of Social Credit supporters but also containing some Liberals and Tories in its ranks. While opponents of the NPA privately acknowledge that the alliance is not all Socreds, they delight nonetheless in referring to the NPA board members as the Socred Farm Team. Aspiring Socred provincial politicians have been known to get their start on the school boards.

School board politics in Vancouver provided a sharp contrast with what passed for politics in most cities. Here there was real debate and real differences in the vision of what education should be. And Campbell was in the thick of it. Her acerbic comments and aggressive style were matched wit for wit and jibe for jibe by another colourful board member, Phil Rankin, now a Vancouver immigration lawyer. Rankin remembers their days sitting on opposite sides of the chamber. After briefly admitting that Campbell actually had a sense of humour and that at times they managed to get along, he gives a stinging assessment of Campbell's tenure on the board, where she was a trustee from 1980 to 1982 as well as chair from 1982 to 1984.

"There isn't one positive thing I can say about her period on the board in terms of an initiative that was for education. She supported special programs for the so-called gifted students. But that was nothing new, just part of the old right-wing agenda which said 'Don't waste your money on dullards but spend on those who are doing all right anyway.' She identified with them because she saw herself as a gifted child. I didn't oppose such programs but her constant reference to them as 'gifted' was absolutely typical of her élitism — everyone else was 'ungifted.' As far as policies for ameliorating hardships, like food programs for hungry kids — nothing. She trumpeted her concern for native children but never promoted a single program to meet their special needs. She was against affirmative action because she said it was an insult to women. Her principal role on the board was to implement the Socreds' provincial restraint program. At that she was very adept and enthusiastic."[20]

During the years that COPE had a majority on the board, they implemented many new programs that attempted to respond to the rapidly changing face of Vancouver. English as a second language (ESL) programs were brought in for the many immigrants from Asia and Latin America; special programs were set up for kids with learning disabilities. Susan Davis, a teacher who at the time was working for the Vancouver Elementary School Teachers Association (VESTA), confirms Rankin's harsh assessment of Campbell's tenure on the board. "She certainly didn't have any sympathy for teachers as working people or for the issues that teachers faced in the classroom. She didn't have very much understanding about what the job of teaching was all about, even though she had taught university. She didn't show much interest in finding out, either. Her approach was a management one. She was fond of saying 'Well, the taxpayer expects this, that and the other thing.' But that's just one small part of a trustee's job ... You know, good working conditions for teachers also translate into good learning conditions for students. She felt her allegiance was more to the taxpayer than it was to improving the education system."[21]

Kitty O'Callaghan was another teacher and president of VESTA. She gives Campbell some credit for working hard and growing somewhat into the job. "I think she became concerned and wanted to do the best job. But she just never seemed to understand the needs. If I have twenty-five or thirty kids and one of them is deaf, then I have to write everything down. That's twice as much work. But she just couldn't empathize with the kids or the teachers."[22]

The strongest memories of Campbell's time on the board, however, are of her treatment of people who dared to disagree with her. Rankin recalls that this imperious behaviour went beyond her adversaries to her NPA colleagues on the board. "Even with her own group, she was constantly grandstanding and undermining any [media] coverage they might get because she is a very jealous person and liked to upstage them whenever possible. Even her own NPA people were put off by her but she intimidated them into appointing her chairperson. She can't give credit to anyone else. No ability whatsoever to give credit where credit is due — it's as if giving any praise would reduce the amount of praise she might get."[23]

Campbell's colleagues tend to agree with this assessment. Ken Denike, who was on the NPA slate with Campbell, recalls that she was extremely difficult to work with. In the course of a meeting, she would often change positions that had been agreed on by the NPA. On one occasion, during the Bennett government's first restraint program, they had come to an agreement that they would support the use of a fund from the sale of school lands rather than lay off teachers. "We went into the meeting and Kim just happened to be the first to speak. She immediately attacked the idea of using the fund, exactly the opposite of what we had decided. It was like pulling a lanyard and the cannon turns around and blasts you. In fact we never knew from one moment to the next when she'd be getting up and taking the opposite side."[24]

Denike claims that Campbell was often unable to apply her intellectual ability to simple policy matters. "She was intellectually precious, but not able to string together a set of themes to make any kind of consistent policy. It had to be put together in a neat, saleable package for her to deliver it and once that had been done, great, she would use almost exactly the same words thereafter, like she had learned her lines. She could learn and present a beautiful, articulate position for a certain context but unfortunately the context may not fit the circumstances."[25]

Campbell consistently took every disagreement with her as a personal slight. Kitty O'Callaghan, as president of VESTA, made several presentations to the board. "There were times when Kim got frustrated with me personally as the leader of the union and at one point said I was just trying to embarrass her publicly. She took personally virtually any issue that was raised."[26]

Campbell's temper was sometimes close to uncontrollable. Denike comments, "She used to get into real arguments with Rankin and she told him to fuck off one time. He knew how to push her buttons. You learned pretty quickly which buttons to push. We had to take her out of situations sometimes because she would short circuit. Someone would almost have to physically calm her down."[27]

The Vancouver school board has one of the most democratic structures of any in the country. Campbell has taken credit for its committee structure, which involves unions, teachers, administrators, parents — everyone with an interest in education. Susan Davis takes exception to that claim, pointing out that it was in place long before Campbell became a trustee. "It was implemented by TEAM — The Electors Action Movement, a civic party in the mid-seventies — when it had a majority on the board. She recently talked about her time on the board as an example of her 'inclusiveness,' implying that she had set up the structure."[28]

While she never objected to the openness of the board structure and meetings, Campbell's attitude was less than inclusive, according to Denike. "Her claim to being a democrat is pretty weak. She was highly supportive of the Bennett government and had a style to match it: hierarchical, top-down, a real hegemony of the professional."[29] According to Rankin, "The previous chair of the board had been very informal and everyone, staff included, operated on a first name basis. The contrast was amazing. She intimidated the hell out of everyone. She frightened people. In reality she made our officials into a bunch of grovelling fools."[30]

Campbell often ridiculed people who made presentations before the board. "I can remember her dressing down the superintendent of schools, in front of all the other deputy superintendents, the parents' association, the teachers' association, at a public meeting, saying to him 'That's absolute rubbish.' I didn't mind her going after another politician but this was pure bullying — he couldn't defend himself — she was his boss."[31] She treated everyone equally — with a snobbish arrogance that often came close to abuse. She once dismissed a parents' association query about why the budget discussions were held in secret with the comment that the queries "were smarmy at best."[32]

None of the people who worked with her on the board, none of the community representatives who dealt with her fully understood why she was there. None, including her colleagues, could identify any educational issue, other than the narrow one of programs for gifted children, that she pursued with any passion or even interest. Even Denike felt that his own NPA under Campbell had failed to make an impact. "There was a whole number of things, hungry kids, English as a second language, that were being totally ignored. Under her chairmanship they were not adequately addressed at all. She simply didn't understand the plight of inner-city kids."[33] People who knew her on the board speculated that her activities there seemed to be a stepping stone to other political goals. It was not long before she proved them right.

Trying Out for the Big League

When Campbell finished her law degree in 1983, she was still chair of the school board. She looked for a law firm to article with. The one she found was one of the largest and most prestigious in the city: Ladner Downs. It was broadly based — mostly conservative and corporate-oriented, but with some labour lawyers as well. Tory David Camp — son of Dalton and a figure who would play prominently in Campbell's political future — was with the firm at the time. He recalls that the firm's partners were concerned that Campbell might not have a long-term commitment to the practice of law. She reassured them by promising to resign as chair of the school board. A few weeks later she announced that she was running for the Social Credit Party in the provincial election to be held in May of that year.[34]

By entering provincial politics with the Socreds in 1983, Campbell was getting in on the ground floor of the most profound political change to hit Canada since the social movements of the mid and late sixties. That she chose Social Credit, and not the Conservatives or Liberals, demonstrated that she was to the right of these political parties at that time and that she went to where the power was.

As it happened, the Social Credit in British Columbia in the early eighties was the testing ground for the federal Conservative and corporate assault on the long-standing social contract that had persisted in Canadian political culture for two generations. It also tested a new generation of political manipulators and pollsters whose techniques and disregard for political integrity would set the standard for the 1980s and 1990s assault on democracy. For someone who valued tradition and the rule of the élite, for someone eager to turn the clock back on a decade of unwanted change, Campbell's timing was perfect. She had always bristled at Phil Rankin's taunts about the Socred farm team, but she had an explanation. She told him, "The party has come around to my way of thinking."[35] Rankin thinks this comment is an example of Campbell's arrogance. But as it turned out, it may have had some truth in it. Campbell's intellectual snobbery initially prevented her from embracing the Socreds' embarrassing populism, but by the time she formally joined the party its parochialism was in the process of being jettisoned for a much more serious image.

Although Campbell lost this particular election, in the course of it she met the men who would transform Bill Bennett from an anti-intellectual small businessman into what Allan Garr called the Tough Guy and show him how to baffle and beat B.C. NDP Leader Dave Barrett.[36] These men would help Brian Mulroney and, just ten years later, they would be at Campbell's side guiding her into the prime minister's job. Lost election or not, it was Campbell's first serious move into the political big leagues.

The Politics of the New Right

The mid-seventies saw a lot of activity among the corporate élite of the developed countries. They were concerned at the direction that governments were taking and the impact of previously marginal groups on public affairs. Prime Minister Pierre Trudeau, Quebec premier René Lévesque, and three NDP provincial governments, in addition to the social movements that successfully lobbied them, had taken much of the control of government away from where it had been for years: in the hands of big business. Big business wanted it back. It began to plan just how to do that.

Among the organizations launched to accomplish this were the Trilateral Commission (which did a study concluding that there was an "excess of democracy"), the Business Round Table in the United States, the Business Council on National Issues (BCNI) in Ottawa and the Fraser Institute in British Columbia. All these organizations played the game slightly differently and with vastly different amounts of power but the broad goal was the same: to restrain the state from intervening on behalf of "interest groups."

B.C. businessmen were especially irritated at the election of a socialist government under Dave Barrett in 1973. They set about planning how to get rid of him. One of the men they talked to was Michael Walker. Although Walker for years was ridiculed as a right-wing crank, nonetheless he had a brilliant insight for those men: "If you really want to change the world you have to change the ideological fabric of the world ... And the way policy gets changed is by creating an ethos in which politicians will see it is in their interest to make these kind of choices."[37] The businessmen took his advice and gave him $200,000 to start up the Fraser Institute, his right-wing think tank. As with the BCNI, it would be almost ten years before the Fraser Institute and its leader Michael Walker would have the impact they set out to have.

Two of the key creators of the new ethos were Patrick Kinsella and Gerry Lampert — experienced operators from the Big Blue Machine of Ontario premier Bill Davis but newcomers to British Columbia. They had connections not only with Ontario Tories but south of the border. "We as Conservatives have a working relationship with the Republican Party in the United States. That allowed me to go to [their] campaign schools, candidate colleges and so on. And frankly I stole all their ideas," boasted Kinsella.[38]

Kinsella and Lampert were part of the talent that Hugh Harries, the new Socred executive director, was buying up to plan Bill Bennett's next election victory. The three men quickly got down to business. The first thing they needed, said Kinsella, was more polling, but of a different kind. The different kind would be provided by the Tory whiz-kids Ian McKinnon and Allan Gregg of Decima Research. They were the hottest pair of political number crunchers in the country, according to political analyst Allan Garr, and they replaced Martin Goldfarb, Bennett's trusted pollster, for most of the important political polling. As Kinsella put it: "Goldfarb only believes that he can take [a poll result] ... and develop a strategy around it. And what ... Decima believes [is] that you can take [poll results] ... and we can change your mind. We can move you to do something that you may not have agreed on is the logical thing to do ... We can move you to the other side of the ledger."[39]

It was the beginning of what Garr called "political genetics." First, they had to change Bill Bennett and the image of the Socreds. That was Hugh Harries's legacy. He "turned a discombobulated bunch of up-country, West Coast loonies into a vital part of the urban, conservative strategy and talent network that spans the continent. He took Bill Bennett out of the country, and he assembled the parts for the Baby Blue Machine that would confidently clobber the NDP in 1983. It would be B.C.'s first taste of 'high tech' politics."[40]

It was marketing technique all the way, as Patrick Kinsella would explain a year later to an audience at Simon Fraser University. The Socreds had a problem, explained Kinsella, because their leader was not nearly as attractive or effective as Dave Barrett, who was friendly, had good relationships with the media and had his party behind him. "He was frankly the kind of guy that you would take to a Canucks game."

Bennett, on the other hand, you would not take to a Canucks game. "The problem was one of marketing. How do you market a guy who ... is seen to be less friendly and less likeable?" The answer was that you convince people that being likeable was not relevant. "In tough times you needed a tough leader. More than ever before what you need is a guy who understands that it's tough out there and he's tough as well. By contrast, surely now we don't need someone who thinks the whole thing is a joke. Now that is taking it to extremes but that's what we tried to get you to believe, if you will, as a voter in 1982–83. And it worked."[41]

Bennett's slogan was "restraint." Allan Garr wrote: "Government services would be chopped and channelled to complement Bill Bennett's Tough Guy image. Power and rights would be removed from children, tenants, school boards, minorities, and trade unions by a tough guy in tough times. The people of B.C. would be set up to believe that what they needed was ... a tough, inflexible son of a bitch they wouldn't be caught dead with at a Canucks hockey game. Toughness was sold as a virtue. Nice meant weak. Restraint was a sado-masochistic exercise: The tougher Bill Bennett got, the better you felt."[42]

Most important, none of the details of this plan would be made part of the campaign platform. The specific plan was by definition a secret plan to be revealed only in its implementation. The strategy was retroactive consensus: Implement sweeping, painful changes at the beginning of your term and by the next election people will have forgotten.

The marketing strategy worked. Behind in the polls by 8 percent when he called the election, Bill Bennett won in May 1983. The marketing techniques that won for him were now a part of

Canadian political culture. The process of "changing the ideological fabric of the world" had begun.

Campbell remembered the restraint campaign and the "tough love" approach when she was running for the leadership ten years later.

Running on Restraint

When Campbell told Phil Rankin that she had joined the Socreds because they had come around to her way of thinking, one suspects that she had restraint in mind. Campbell was an ideological conservative, and up to the point when Hugh Harries, Patrick Kinsella and Gerry Lampert took over the marketing of the Socreds, there was no party that fit her Burkean view of government by the élite or that took conservatism seriously. If there was, certainly there was none that could actually win. Her contempt for the "rabble," amply demonstrated on the school board, also applied to the right-wing populism and small-town "good-old-boys" politics of the old Bill Bennett.

But the new Bill Bennett would have been to her liking. He was beginning, in 1982, to sound like a conservative. Norman Spector was in charge of prepping the premier. "[Bill Bennett] was being injected with the latest in neo-conservative language. When Norman Spector read Milton Friedman, Bill Bennett talked about the tyranny of the minorities, when Norman Spector picked up Mancur Olson, Bill Bennett started to make speeches about special interest groups."[43] Campbell was impressed.

If Campbell needed a little persuasion to take the leap into provincial politics, she could hardly have had a more influential mentor than Patrick Kinsella. He recognized in Campbell someone who had the right politics for the new Socred era. He asked her to run against Gary Lauk, the NDP incumbent, in the two-seat riding of Vancouver Centre. She accepted, although she told David Camp that she did not expect to win.

Nevertheless, she wanted to be part of the election in 1983. Lauk describes Campbell as "a very right-wing conservative politician. She's not a Flora MacDonald or Joe Clark. She's a Thatcherite. The campaign showed that on social policy issues and all of the economic issues she is very right wing. She thinks of herself as a true-blue rightist. So she loved the restraint program and took it up in her campaign with real enthusiasm."[44]

Lauk, like Rankin, had some grudging admiration for Campbell. "She's a vigorous, very aggressive politician and I don't think that's necessarily a bad thing. She was a good sport." But Lauk also remembers Campbell's tendency to lose her temper. Lauk uses the same phrase as Rankin to describe how easy it was to make her angry. "I loved to push her political buttons during the campaign — she was so easily rattled. She would get hysterical. It was so predictable that we stopped doing it because it became too obvious. The finger-wagging, the high-pitched voice. Maybe she's changed."[45]

Lauk was never in serious trouble and the campaign was relatively uneventful. One incident, however, seemed to secure the vote for the NDPer. One of Campbell's campaign workers sent out a letter to all the landlords in the riding, telling them a vote for Lauk meant rent controls but that a vote for Campbell would mean that they would be able to raise their rents right away. Lauk published the letter in the local community newspaper, which came out just two days before the election. The rent control letter was a revealing slip: Campbell and her workers obviously knew what was in store regarding the secret legislative agenda. And they were right not to reveal it. Says Lauk, "We'd have won anyway but the letter really hurt her. I don't think that Kim Campbell has very good judgement about people, and she doesn't have very many friends."[46]

Campbell lost by a two-to-one margin, but in the process she had staked out her ground as a committed right-wing politician. And she met many of the Tory heavyweights that would influence and help her in the years ahead: Norman Spector, Hugh Segal, Gerry Lampert and pollster Allan Gregg. She was not in the main room of the new Tory politics, but she was just outside the door waiting for the next invitation. In the meantime she would prove her restraint credentials on the school board.

Bill Bennett's Blitzkrieg

Bill Bennett's government brought down its first budget shortly after its election victory. It contained cuts that everyone expected and while some were severe, most were described as "budgetary adjustments." They did not sound any alarm bells. But in the legislative chambers, instead of introducing the handful of enabling bills, as was usually the case, suddenly minister after minister rose with rehearsed precision and introduced bill after bill.[47] The NDP opposition and the reporters in the budget lock-up were caught off guard and were suddenly buried in an avalanche of legislation. As the reporters began to read through the bills, the enormity of what the Socreds were planning began to sink in.

It was a massive sneak attack. The Socreds had fired all their guns at once. In the next few days all the details were known across the province. Two hundred thousand civil servants were put on notice that they could be fired without cause once their agreement expired. Seniority disappeared. The government said it was going to eliminate 25 percent of the civil service. Tax credits for the elderly and for tenants were eliminated. All budget making by local school boards was cancelled. Regional districts' zoning authority was gone; civil servants' wages could be rolled back; the Minister of Education now had control over what courses and programs would be offered or cancelled at the B.C. Institute of Technology; virtually all college advisory boards were eliminated. The Employment Standards Amendment Act allowed employers to sign contracts below the established provincial minimum employment standards and the Employment Standards Act was wiped out — workers with complaints would now have to go to court. Rent controls were gone; landlords could evict without cause.

The Human Rights Branch and Commission were on a special hit list. Allan Garr writes: "With orders from Victoria and a command post within the ministry of labour office in Burnaby, hit men fan out across the province. Seven regional Human Rights Branch offices are shut down on Friday, July 8, and the locks are changed. Ken Chamberlain is a Socred flunky. July 8, 1983, is his finest hour.

"Two women are sitting at their desks when Chamberlain enters the Vancouver office of the Human Rights Commission ... Chamberlain, a total stranger to them, hands them their termination notices and gives them fifteen minutes to clear out their desks, take their personal belongings, hand over their office keys and get out."[48] It was a scene repeated across the province, and not just in human rights.

While tens of thousands of ordinary British Columbians were experiencing everything from trauma to insecurity for their futures under Bennett's massive assault, one man was basking in his glory. Michael Walker of the Fraser Institute, after enduring ten years of obscurity, ridicule and marginality was seeing his neo-conservative revolution unfold before his very eyes. In a column he wrote a few days after the legislation came down, Walker joyously congratulated the government for abandoning rent controls; the firing of government workers "without cause" was even better. Most important was the government's big bang approach: "There is nothing known about how to implement a policy of restraint; there is something known about how special interest groups respond."[49]

Part of the political strategy was the deliberate polarization of B.C. society — something that was not difficult to do. There would be no apologies for the attack on the "tyranny of the minority." Bennett referred to those who protested the restraint program as the "coalition of dissent" and labelled anyone who disagreed with his policies "bad British Columbians."[50]

Bennett's strategy of polarizing the province worked beyond his wildest dreams. The restraint program set off an explosion of protest that was heard across the country and the continent. Within weeks, virtually every group affected by the Bennett onslaught — and there were hundreds, in dozens of communities — had begun mobilizing against the government. The resistance soon became known as Operation Solidarity. It organized the most massive protest movement the country had seen in decades. Marches and demonstrations of tens of thousands of people became commonplace.

The confrontation between Solidarity and the Socreds was no mere "polarization"; it was the closest thing to class warfare that Canada had seen since the 1930s. Ian Mulgrew of *The Globe and Mail* wrote five months later: "Class warfare used to be a joke in this province. In the spring of 1984 no one is laughing."[51]

For 130 days the confrontation raged and grew. Until the last moment, it seemed as though the much-talked-about general strike would actually happen. But in the end, despite the enormous energy, anger and effort to resist Bennett's program, Solidarity was defeated. The NDP, humiliated and dumbfounded by its election defeat and terrified, as always, by radical expressions beyond its control, pouted in Victoria while Solidarity became the only real opposition. The NDP simply did not understand the long-term implications of Bennett's plan.

But more importantly, it was the NDP's labour arm that in the end got cold feet at the idea of actually exercising its ultimate weapon — the general strike — for the general good. In the showdown with Bill Bennett, Norman Spector and Patrick Kinsella, the labour bureaucrats blinked and Solidarity died.

A Bit Part

Campbell was not destined to serve in Bill Bennett's government in the B.C. legislature. But she would play her bit part on the Vancouver school board with enthusiasm. She clearly saw herself as part of the Socred team and a defender of its agenda. She had been persuaded to run for the party precisely because Patrick Kinsella and the others on the team of neo-conservative whiz-kids had transformed Bill Bennett into a serious conservative like herself. Campbell's early connection with Kinsella leaves little doubt that she was fully aware of the Socreds' unstated agenda. Her over-enthusiastic campaign worker let the cat out of the bag when he promised landlords a free hand in raising their rents. There was no indication that she disagreed with any of Bennett's actions, including the centrepiece of his political attack: the destruction of the Human Rights Commission and the government Human Rights Branch. "Rights" were a favourite target for conservatives, and as Campbell would demonstrate later, she shared their hostility to the concept. One of the key "interest groups" targeted by Bennett personally was the teachers. Bennett had never forgiven the teachers for their key role in the defeat of his father, W.A.C. "Wacky" Bennett, in 1973. The restraint program was a perfect excuse to take his revenge. In fact, he had already unleashed a brutal attack on education in 1982. Budget cuts to education would eventually result in the lay-off of over 4,000 teachers. As chair of the Vancouver school board, Campbell was in a position to help Bennett.

Virtually all those involved with the school board in the post-election period testify to one thing: Campbell's continued dedication to the Socred restraint program was virtually her only goal as board chair. Her NPA colleague, Ken Denike, saw her as little more than a stalking horse for the Socred government. "She was in a sense an apologist for the Bennett government."[52]

Campbell was not content simply to acquiesce to restraint; she bragged about how dedicated she was to the government's program. In refusing to defend the Vancouver school board's budget from the planned cuts, she called the reduced figure "socially responsible." In an interview she stated, "[The budget] takes restraint seriously ... We've expressed sincerity to the provincial government, we're not thumbing our noses at restraint."[53] When the numerous groups involved in the advisory committees were asked to make suggestions about how to respond to the budget cuts, Campbell was annoyed that they called for defending the programs instead of naming those to be cut. Susan Davis recalls: "We all got publicly bawled out for not having produced anything useful to the board in terms of where it should cut its budget. But we were advocating for the system — it wasn't our job to help them cut our own programs. We weren't going to say it's all right if you cut off our left hand because we can write perfectly well with our right."[54]

For her part, Campbell had no intention of apologizing for publicly rebuking the parents and teachers for their contributions. Reinforcing her reputation for snobbish superiority, she told the Vancouver *Sun,* "I think it had to be said. I think it was true. Let us not delude ourselves as to what was going on. You have these little charades that take place and everybody is playing their role. That baffles me. It offends my sense of integrity." If this snobbishness bothered people, that was their problem, suggested Campbell. "I have discovered that I don't need to be loved by the public."[55]

Teachers, parents, administrators and employee groups asked Campbell to defend education. According to Davis, "They were saying, 'Look, these are the needs of the system. We want you to at least express this to the government.' She wasn't interested. She looked down on us and commented that our proposals were 'marginally useful.' "[56] Ken Denike became chair of the board after the next board election. "It wasn't until a new board was elected that we were able to address [some of the real education issues] and to fight for, and get, more funding from the government. We had to do some pretty heavy lobbying."[57]

The confrontation between Operation Solidarity — the mass opposition to the Bennett cuts — and the government reached its critical point when teachers hit the picket lines. Fewer than 60 percent voted in favour of the strike and almost everyone — certainly the government — believed that if the teachers' leadership called them out, the strike would flop. Instead, the teachers, angry at being so hard-hit for so long, responded with a 90 to 95 percent turnout. The hoped-for general strike was a big step closer.

Campbell acted immediately, applying for an injunction to stop the strikers from setting up picket lines — a move designed by Socred strategists to allow the less committed among the teachers to go in to work without having to confront their colleagues. In a widely reported attack on her own teachers, Campbell declared that what they needed was a "kick in the ass." She was overheard referring to them as "terrorists holding us all to ransom."[58]

Susan Davis still remembers Campbell's remarks vividly. "I thought at the time, 'What an incredibly coarse, crass thing to say for someone holding public office.' I found her to be, generally, a very common person, often coarse and rude." Yet despite the implication of Campbell's remark, the teachers' strike had nothing to do with salaries. Those were determined by binding arbitration. The teachers were striking for education. As Davis explained, "In those days teachers had never gone on a job action, they just didn't see themselves that way. The strike was a political protest. We were protesting legislation drastically affecting education. The legislation was so vicious and repressive — nothing else would have got the teachers out. They were scared but they were even more angry."[59]

Ken Denike remembers Campbell's attitude towards the striking teachers as being quite different from that of others in the NPA group. "She took the strike really personally, which was a real problem. I don't think an elected person can take those things personally if you can help it."[60]

Gary Lauk, Campbell's NDP opponent in the 1983 election, found Campbell to be much more vigorously anti-union than even most Social Credit supporters. "On three or four occasions [when there were public service strikes] she spoke out. When the teachers were out and city workers were striking she was stridently anti-union. Even the middle-of-the-road politicians of her own party weren't blatantly anti-union. But she was really strident about it, which struck me as odd for [that period]. But then, she was particularly bloodthirsty when it came to restraint, especially since [the province] wasn't facing a particularly tough time financially."[61]

Moving Onwards and Upwards

Campbell stayed with Ladner Downs through 1984. But she soon confirmed the fear of the firm's partners that she had little commitment to her profession other than as an opening to politics. In 1985, Bill Bennett invited her into his government as a policy advisor in his office, with the title of executive director. She leaped at the chance.

Bennett's operation was, like his government, lean. There were only three senior people who worked closely with him: new-right ideological guru Norman Spector, who was deputy minister; Bud Smith, the principal secretary who eventually became a Socred cabinet minister; and Campbell. It was Smith who approached Campbell to join Bennett's office. He recalls that Campbell was one of the few politicians at the time who really understood the fundamentals of the neo-conservative agenda. "She exhibited a profound understanding of the importance of having a long-term conservative view of fiscal management. She had no difficulty at all in selling restraint."[62]

Very little has been written about the specifics of Campbell's job in Bennett's office, and Campbell herself has rarely talked about it. She worked with Bennett for only a year, barely enough time to get adjusted to her responsibilities. According to Bud Smith, she worked on two assignments for Bennett: a wilderness advisory committee that was intended to draw up plans for land use in the province's forests, and a re-examination of aboriginal land claims. The Socred position on the issue — refusal to recognize the legitimacy of such claims — was becoming increasingly untenable in the mid-eighties.

Bennett, says Smith, liked Campbell, "gave her a lot of time" and was impressed with her. But neither of Campbell's efforts bore fruit before Bennett surprised most people, including many of those close to him, by stepping down in 1986. By doing so, he threw the whole neo-conservative agenda, so carefully planned and executed by Spector, Kinsella and a few others, into doubt. Kinsella, the self-described "best political hack in the country," was already gone: "The name of the game is to win." Having won, he headed east, intent on either helping Bill Davis in Ontario or ensuring that Joe Clark did not retain the Tory leadership.[63] Spector soon followed. He and the others could not be sure that the next leader of the Socreds would be such a willing student of their "political genetics" as Bill Bennett had been.

Kim Campbell, Leadership Hopeful

With Bennett gone, Campbell's job was gone. She was faced with remaining in politics or returning to the legal career she had never really started. Campbell announced her choice to remain in the political world of Social Credit in a bizarre move that startled virtually everyone. Campbell, who had never been an MLA, had run for the party only once and that only three years earlier, and with no base of support, put her name forward for the leadership of the party.

David Camp, who in 1983 had raised questions about her running for a seat when she had just joined the law firm, again tried to intervene. Her candidacy simply made no sense. He predicted correctly that she would come in last.[64] Grace McCarthy, the powerhouse of the Socreds who was given credit for rebuilding the party after its defeat in 1973, believed at the time that Campbell may have been put up to it. "I thought it was a set-up to take [the leadership] away from me."[65]

Running for the leadership could be seen in two ways — as a bold move to establish herself for a future run or just another expression of Campbell's ego. Rankin's assessment of her leaves no doubt as to where he stands on the question. "She's a megalomaniac of such proportions that she could be clinically diagnosed — a lot like Mulroney. She has an insatiable ego, a desperate need to be somebody."[66] Campbell's own explanation suggests that she was simply increasing her political recognition for a more serious move later on. "Many people feel I gave the campaign some legitimacy. There were two winners ... One was Bill Vander Zalm and the other was me — mainly because of the luck of the draw." For her speech, Campbell drew the number ten spot out of twelve candidates, and the last two just happened to end up being the last two on the final ballot — Bill Vander Zalm and Brian Smith. "There was a big T.V. audience ... In terms of getting out the message that I had to deliver, I got a pretty good hearing."[67]

Campbell finished last of twelve candidates and received only fourteen votes. But she did leave her mark with a stinging and prescient barb thrown at the new premier, Bill Vander Zalm. No doubt irritated at the prospect of a leader even more buffoonish than the pre-Kinsella Bennett had been, she warned the delegates: "Charisma without substance is a dangerous thing." It was a one-liner destined to become famous — and to come back to haunt her in 1993. But it served her well. Despite her last-place finish, she got high marks from many observers for having given the best speech at the convention.

Her "charisma without substance" comment was not all that she became famous for during her leadership race. In an interview with Gillian Shaw of the Vancouver *Sun,* Campbell's famous "candour" got her into trouble. Campbell revealed to Shaw that she saw herself as a natural leader whose role it was to "enlighten" people and "foster growth." As for the common people: "I think it is important to realize that a lot of people that you're out there working for are people who may sit in their undershirt and watch the game on Saturday, beer in hand." Campbell stated that she liked to socialize with her own, "intellectually oriented" people and not the game-watchers and beer drinkers. "I suppose they would find me as boring as I would them. A lot of their attitudes you may not agree with, but they come from genuine human emotions. If you don't understand that and like people ... you can't take them anywhere."[68]

In 1986 Campbell remarried, having divorced Nathan Divinsky in 1983. Her second husband was Howard Eddy, a lawyer she met while working in Bennett's office. A quiet, reserved former UBC law professor, Eddy was most noted for being the Social Credit government's principal front-line lawyer fighting aboriginal land claims. The Socreds' position on aboriginal rights was straightforward. They did not exist. Eddy spearheaded the province's strategy "to stop courts from recognizing the existence of aboriginal rights."

In the 1986 provincial election, Campbell won a seat in the legislature in one of the double-member ridings in Vancouver's Point Grey area. The other member was NDPer Darlene Marzari. "During the election — and later in the house — she espoused a good, neo-conservative line all the time. As far as community issues were concerned, such as economic issues and the Indian reserve in the area, she was a Tory: there was no flexibility. She promoted small business and megaprojects. Her line was and remains a conservative agenda. That's certainly the face she has presented back to B.C."[69]

Although Campbell had apparently been working for Bennett on changing the government's approach to aboriginal land claims, Marzari remembers her taking the official Socred position. "She took the Socred line on native status in B.C. It was the last province in the country to recognize the Indians' right to official status. She opposed that throughout her time as a Socred. The government refused to recognize the Indians' right even to file a claim. They simply refused to sit down at the table because there was nothing to negotiate."[70] Marzari's recollection was confirmed by a poll of the candidates taken earlier that year by the Vancouver *Sun*. Asked whether or not she would initiate aboriginal land claims with the native population, Campbell replied, "No. I'm persuaded by the province's position on land claims."[71]

Once Campbell got into the house, she discovered how lonely and tedious life could be as a backbencher, for that was to be her lot under Vander Zalm. Her criticism of him at the convention and her reputation as an "intellectual" finished off any consideration of Campbell for a cabinet post. Nonetheless, said McCarthy, "Under anyone else's administration she would have been a cabinet minister, she should have been."[72]

While Campbell's backbench status kept her largely out of the limelight and revealed little about her political philosophy or vision of the country, one small incident is worth recording. Philip Resnick, a political science professor at the University of British Columbia, attended a meeting with the two MLAs Campbell and Marzari. Campbell spoke up in strong defence of two anti-union bills the government had introduced. Resnick reminded her that during the election there had been talk by the Socreds about the need for reconciliation and healing of the wounds caused by the confrontation of 1983 — and pointed out that there had been no consultation with labour on the new legislation. "Her reply was very revealing of her view of democracy," said Resnick. "She said, 'In a democracy, the way it works is the winning side gets to introduce its program. We won and we are introducing our program.' End of discussion. I interpret that as a real contradiction of her talk about 'inclusiveness.' Her record and her statement reveal a very hard, neo-conservative politics. No olive branches, no apologies, no recognition at all of a need for some kind of minimal consensus. The answer she gave me was a perfect summary of the kind of politics she stood for."[73]

Campbell languished for two years on the Socred back benches, serving on policy committees and doing work on heritage preservation and cultural policy. It was clearly a political dead-end. Vander Zalm had no intention of promoting her. In February 1988 she ensured her place on the back benches with another attack on the premier. This time it was over abortion.

Vander Zalm, with no consultation with his caucus and no warning, announced that the government would no longer fund abortions through the medicare plan. Campbell broke with Vander Zalm at the time and a month later went even further. The Vancouver *Sun* reported that "Campbell warned that personal convictions based on a 'narrow bigoted opinion' are dangerous when they are used by politicians to force their moral views on the rest of the population."[74] Stating that the caucus wanted a say on this controversial issue, she called on Vander Zalm to show statesmanship. She added: "I don't believe all convictions are created equal ... He's glamorized his convictions but his convictions are full of it."[75]

Grace McCarthy believes that Campbell initiated the dispute with Vander Zalm over abortion as a convenient way to escape a dead-end role on the back benches with a premier who did not like her. "She wasn't going anywhere, why would she stay?"[76] Planned or otherwise, it marked the end of Campbell's phase as a Social Crediter.

The Politics of Inclusion?

Kim Campbell's reasons for joining the Conservative Party and leaping into the "free trade election" of 1988 are simply stated. She could not abide John Turner's "dishonest" attack on the Canada–U.S. Free Trade Agreement. Her "public duty" demanded that she abandon her seat in the B.C. legislature and run for the Tories.

Campbell heard Turner speak at a municipalities convention in Whistler. She claimed, "I sat in the audience and realized that the people around me had no basis to judge what he was saying ... I couldn't stay outside that fight."[1] She referred to this incident several times: "I couldn't believe what I was hearing — it really curled my hair. This wasn't the old, bumbling John Turner."[2] And in another interview: "I heard him completely distort the free trade agreement and say things that I think were completely misleading. It really kind of frightened me. There is really a fear campaign going on and I think it's unbelievably damaging and it hurts the integrity of the political process."[3]

Although Campbell claimed that she was joining the Tories to help crusade against the anti–free trade lobby, there was no doubt an element of opportunism. It was obvious that Campbell was not happy with her lot in the back benches of the Socred government. Tex Enemark, her Liberal opponent in Vancouver Centre, had also joined the campaign late in the game. A one-time aide to Liberal cabinet minister Ron Basford, Enemark observed: "When she said that she entered the race because she couldn't let Turner's 'outrageous comments' go unchallenged, that was just typical Kim Campbell hyperbole. No one took it seriously."[4]

Stories circulating at the time suggested that her decision to run was considerably more complicated. It was public knowledge that Campbell had been approached to run against John Turner in Vancouver Quadra but had turned down the offer because the odds against her were too steep. Rumours in political and media circles suggest that initially Campbell resisted efforts to recruit her to the

Tory cause. However impatient she was with the existing situation with Vander Zalm, the argument went, Campbell was confident that there would be a changing of the guard in the province in a few years. She felt well placed to take advantage of that likelihood. She was also building towards a pension as an MLA and did not want to abandon that with nothing to fall back on. To help persuade her, the Tories allegedly put together a $65,000 care package as compensation for her lost pension benefits, her lost salary as an MLA and lost income for the time that she spent running in the campaign.

There was never proof of the allegations. In any case, Campbell used the "Turner challenge" gambit to her advantage. And it was clear that the party saw her as the leader of the fight for free trade in the province, as well as someone who could distance them from Vander Zalm. As Thomas Walkom wrote in *The Globe and Mail,* "A renegade Social Credit legislator has become the great blond hope for Brian Mulroney's embattled British Columbia Tories. They think Kim Campbell can distance the federal party from controversial Premier William Vander Zalm. They are also looking for her to counter widespread opposition to free trade in the province."[5] There was no disagreement with this analysis from the Tories. Her campaign organizer, Lyall Knott, declared that Campbell became "*the* B.C. spokesperson for the trade deal overnight."[6]

In Campbell's acceptance speech at her nomination as the new Progressive Conservative candidate for Vancouver Centre — she ran unopposed and was introduced by Pat Carney, who was not running again — she won cheers from the crowd with her denunciation of the NDP and the Liberals. She attacked both Turner and the NDP's Ed Broadbent for their "cynicism and hypocrisy" in opposing free trade. "Canadians must reject the appeals of those political leaders 'Jingo John' and 'Oshawa Ed' who wrap themselves in the flag while they not only sell Canadians short but sell them out," said Campbell. "The incredible fear-mongering and distortion which have characterized the discussions of the free-trade agreement in this campaign illustrates clearly their fear of exposure. Canadians deserve better than the hysterical deception they are getting from the Liberals and the NDP."[7]

Her nastiness and sarcasm were not reserved just for Turner and Broadbent. She also went after Dave Barrett, the former NDP premier who was running for a federal seat in Esquimalt-Juan de Fuca. "The one and only NDP premier of B.C. has rushed back to

contest this election and fight against free trade — rushed back
from where — Cambridge, Mass., where he was glad to take U.S.
dollars to teach the intellectual philistines of Harvard University
about the virtues of socialism."[8]

There was really only one issue in the campaign and that was
the Canada–U.S. Free Trade Agreement. Efforts at bringing other
issues into the spotlight were few and far between and rarely
reported by the media. Some found Campbell's approach high-
handed. She seemed to imply that no one else knew anything
about the deal. Tex Enemark was left shaking his head at Campbell's personal attacks and élitist approach. "Kim is very much
above the rest of us. She kind of looks down on us. She has a firm
grasp of the whole truth, that's the impression she gives. Everybody else is either stupid or a liar."[9]

Campbell herself more than hinted that the Liberals and NDP
were liars. "I'm a parliamentarian and you know how hard it is to
use the word lie," Campbell told the Victoria *Times Colonist*. She
then went on to describe her opponents' use of the "big lie"
technique, "and it's a lie they tell to win support in southern
Ontario."[10]

Enemark describes one disturbing incident in the campaign. "It
was a very dirty campaign. I can remember senior Vancouver
lawyers lining up to jeer John Turner who had come to speak at
the Hotel Vancouver. We had to walk through a large public area
to get to the ballroom where he was speaking. As Turner passed,
these senior lawyers yelled, 'Liar, liar, liar, liar!' I had been
involved in politics for thirty years at that point and if I could have
left politics right then and resigned my candidacy I would have
done so. I have never been so disgusted in my life as I was that
night. These were all lawyers involved in Campbell's campaign
— I knew them all — and they had a bunch of young people with
them, who didn't know any better, I suppose. It just reminded me
too much of the awful, negative politics of U.S. elections. It really
brought Kim down a few notches in my estimation."[11]

Johanna den Hertog was the NDP's candidate in Vancouver
Centre in the 1988 election and had been widely expected to win
the seat after working the riding for six months. Den Hertog found
Campbell "loud, aggressive and accusatory"[12] in debates with her
during the campaign. She acknowledges Campbell's intelligence
as well as her arrogance: "She gets very hostile with opponents
when they challenge her arguments."[13]

Campbell did not restrict the ferocious style of her defence of the Mulroney trade deal to her rival candidates. She became famous for her red-faced screaming attack on hecklers at the first public candidates' meeting of the election. "What are you people afraid of!" she screamed repeatedly into the microphone as anti-free traders heckled her speech. According to Enemark, the heckling only began after Campbell supporters — "a bunch of Tory brownshirts" — had shouted down Johanna den Hertog "with Campbell's encouragement."[14] The meeting revealed Campbell's tendency to lose control if people push her too hard.

"She had abandoned any moral high ground to ask for a fair hearing ... She was on the edge of tears the whole time ... she gets very emotional. She kind of loses her grip on things,"[15] said Enemark, in terms reminiscent of those used by Ken Denike and others who witnessed her frequent outbursts on the Vancouver school board.

Enemark recalls that in the several debates the candidates held on the subject of the trade deal, Campbell's response was always the same: her opponents "didn't know what they were talking about." On one occasion, when the topic shifted away from the deal and on to child care, Campbell took the same tactic, which Enemark described as "bullying."[16]

"The TV host, Jim Hart, asked her about her party's promise of a national child care program. She replied, 'It's not a promise, it's a commitment.' When asked to explain the difference, she replied, 'A promise is a promise, a commitment is a commitment.' I said, 'Wait a minute — a promise refers to something in the future and a commitment is for something that has already been provided for. There's no money in the fiscal framework for this program — and it's too big to be hidden anywhere else.' She just sneered, 'You don't know what you're talking about.' "[17]

Enemark suggests that Campbell knew the details of the trade deal well. If she did, that does not put her in a favourable light regarding her claims for the deal or the basis for her attacks on its critics. She ridiculed Broadbent — "Oshawa Ed" — by claiming that he had a double standard regarding free trade. "[He] warns us of the evils of American investment and American multi-nationals. But he loves General Motors which has invested $8 billion in his riding ... Free trade in the form of the auto pact is fine for Oshawa but not for the rest of the country."[18]

But the auto pact, as all trade experts acknowledged, was not free trade but managed trade: there were guarantees established that tied the number of automobiles built in Canada to the number sold; it was precisely these guarantees that resulted in the billions in investment. The auto pact stipulated that if the U.S. automobile manufacturers wanted to sell their cars here, they had to build them here. The free trade agreement not only had no such provision, but any similar provision for future production in other sectors was explicitly forbidden, according to its terms.

Campbell also vigorously denied that medicare was or would be affected by the free trade agreement. She berated those who attempted to explain the implications for national social programs of the deal's yet-undefined ban on "unfair subsidies." It has not been lost on those who heard her indignant denunciations that by 1993 she was calling for the reconsideration of user fees and an end to universality in medicare — the very things that opponents said would result from the deal.

Campbell made no concessions to those expressing fears about the deal: about loss of jobs, about social programs, about losing control of our energy supplies, about our ability to implement new national programs, about the erosion of environmental and health standards and supply management of agricultural products. All of the fears expressed by those who examined the deal for themselves — whether political figures or those in the groups affected — were lightly dismissed. Her response to the many thousands of Vancouverites and other Canadians who, in retrospect, had every reason to be "afraid" of the deal was: "Ignorance is bliss, I guess. But it's frustrating when you know things about [the FTA] and you see the stupidities. I have to pick and choose which ridiculous statement I answer and that is frustrating."[19]

As polls showed the free trade agreement becoming increasingly unpopular in British Columbia — in early November people were lining up 55 percent against and 23 percent for — Campbell became more strident in its defence, according to the Ottawa *Citizen*'s Iain Hunter. "In all three candidates' debates Campbell has abused her opponents." The Ottawa reporter ended his story by telling readers that Campbell bore the responsibility of filling the shoes of both Pat Carney and John Fraser, now running as non-partisan Speaker of the House. "If she doesn't [succeed]," wrote Hunter, "it won't be for lack of yelling."[20]

Campbell continued to ridicule or simply dismiss the warnings that opponents made about the deal. "If the Americans can have access to our water under the deal we can have access to theirs."[21] She spent more time fending off criticisms of the agreement than arguing its benefits. She did claim one benefit, however: that it met British Columbia's historic quest for lower tariffs. In fact, the forest industry was only grudgingly supportive because it knew full well that the deal did not, as it had sought to do, protect Canadian producers from American trade remedy laws.

Indeed, as Campbell must have known if she knew the agreement at all, it had very little to do with reducing tariffs, especially on goods produced in British Columbia. And her additional promotion of the deal as a boon to B.C. manufacturers wishing to sell to the Los Angeles market was misleading. It was not tariffs that prevented the auto companies from investing in British Columbia. That industry had enjoyed zero tariffs for twenty years as the result of the auto pact, and companies still preferred to set up plants in Ontario.[22]

Vancouver Centre probably got more media attention than any other riding in Western Canada. It had long been identified as a bellwether riding and more often than not sent a cabinet minister to Ottawa. Liberal Ron Basford and Tory Pat Carney were the most recent examples. The race was a close one and Campbell, despite being behind in the polls and starting two weeks late, ran a well-organized campaign, inheriting a strong organization from Pat Carney. Johanna den Hertog, the national president of the NDP, was widely expected to win. Tex Enemark also ran a strong campaign and attributes Campbell's win — she won by just 279 votes — to the strong counter-attack on free trade by the Tories in the final few weeks of the campaign. "Kim Campbell won because Brian Mulroney won," says Enemark.

Lauro de Haan, an activist in the AIDS community in the riding, believes that Campbell rode to victory on the coattails of Pat Carney. "Carney was just an excellent constituency person — very attentive and responsive to anyone who requested her help, whether or not she sympathized with your cause. Campbell definitely benefited from Carney's hard work."[23]

Campbell may have benefited from Pat Carney's record as an attentive constituency person, but by virtually all accounts she has not followed in that tradition. Groups as diverse as parents wanting child care, businessmen needing help with proposed developments, the elderly, people with AIDS, and gays and lesbians are virtually unanimous: once elected, Campbell was extremely hard to reach and rarely, if ever, assisted when asked to. Some constituents called her an absentee MP. But the criticism goes beyond her apparent indifference to the day-to-day problems of constituents. Business people claim that for all her pro-business stance, her promises of great things for the province and her status as the province's senior minister, Campbell has done very little for British Columbia.

Kim Campbell, MP: The Politics of Child Care

Few subjects dogged Campbell during her leadership campaign as much as the child care issue. The Conservative government's decision to cancel a promised national child care program just a few short months after the 1988 election was brought up several times as a challenge to her claim to be a feminist. In response, Campbell stated that a national child care program is just not on: "The kinds of things we looked at in 1988 are just not economically feasible."[24] Yet several times during the 1993 leadership campaign she stated that her social policy will take children into account. "My approach to social policy will be strongly focussed on the interests of children."[25]

Campbell's "children-focussed" approach might come as a surprise to a group of parents in Campbell's own constituency of Vancouver Centre. Approximately eighty parents were caught off-guard in October 1992 when they received notice that their child care/pre-school centre, called Over the Rainbow (OTR), was closing in two months and that they would have to find alternative facilities for their children. The privately run centre, located on Granville Island and serving the Granville Island Market as well as the local neighbourhood, had just had its rent increased by 133 percent and it could no longer afford to stay open. After eight years, a unique child care centre was not simply out of business. It was in effect being forced from its premises by its landlord, the Kids Only Market (KOM), a mall that originally carried only children's merchandise.

The centre was especially useful in that it took children for three hours maximum at a time, twice a week. It was used by shoppers at the market but also by many women who were looking after their children full-time and yet working part-time to keep their careers intact. The pre-school program was especially attractive and the parents felt a strong loyalty to it. They were upset at the centre's closing, and as the days passed after the announcement they became increasingly frustrated in their efforts to find out why it had happened. Part of their frustration resulted from the treatment they received at the hands of Campbell, who adamantly refused to respond to the parents seeking her assistance. This stonewalling on what most saw as a bread-and-butter issue for any MP was inexplicable. It was exacerbated by Campbell's active efforts, through her Vancouver constituency staff, to undermine and discredit the parents.

The Granville Island Market, a major attraction to visitors to Vancouver, is equally popular with the city's residents. Established by the Liberal government of Pierre Trudeau, it was intended to be a mix of commercial enterprises, cultural groups and artisans. The latter two groups pay rent at subsidized rates, while the commercial operations pay full market value. The federal government holds the leases through the Canada Mortgage and Housing Corporation (CMHC). Merchants in the market accept that their higher rents in effect subsidize other activities, in part because this has always been a condition of their lease but also because they know that these activities bring in customers.

Two parents using the child care centre, Janet McPhee and Cherie Miltimore, actively attempted to reverse the eviction of Over the Rainbow. When the closing was first announced, McPhee, Miltimore and other parents went to one of the main actors in the situation to try to get some answers. Barbara Smith, the owner of OTR, was unable to provide any. Smith subleased the space from the Kids Only Market which, in turn, leased it from the CMHC. "Right away we interviewed CMHC people — asking them to help us keep it open. Then we went to Kids Only management to get the facts from their side and really got no satisfaction. We wanted CMHC to give us the phone numbers of the Granville Trust's board members but they refused,"[26] explained Cherie Miltimore. (The Granville Island Trust was the governing body of the island, appointed by the federal government.) That's when the parents went to Campbell.

Janet McPhee phoned first in November: "They initially told me they were very concerned and that Campbell would be pleased to meet with me," says McPhee. "I was to phone her constituency office and get on the waiting list. Then we waited and waited till mid-December and heard nothing." Miltimore was also calling, trying to get some straight answers. "They kept promising me the phone numbers of the trustees — 'We'll fax it Tuesday, we'll fax it this afternoon, we'll fax it Thursday.' They just led us on. Then I found out that Campbell's head staffer, Diana Lam, had phoned Barbara Smith [OTR's owner] and said, 'Get those parents off our back or they'll piss off the public.' I thought it was an odd way for an MP's assistant to deal with us. I finally phoned again and said if you don't want to help us just say so. But from then on Diana Lam refused to ever call us back."[27]

By this time the parents had done some investigating of their own. They discovered that there appeared to be a condition on the lease that prevented KOM from ever renting the child care building at commercial rates. They had been told by KOM that the condition was not in the lease, but knew that it would be in the minutes of the 1984 CMHC meetings at which KOM's proposal had been considered. To establish their claim, the parents approached one of the original developers, who proved willing to sign an affidavit in front of a commissioner of oaths confirming the parents' claim about the condition that the trust had placed on the lease.[28] They also solicited a letter from one of the original board members of the Granville Island Trust, confirming the lease condition.[29]

The parents made the mistake of telling Campbell's staff that they had the affidavit."We were so confident in our facts that we naïvely assumed that people would help us. We faxed the affidavit over to Campbell's office. When we phoned over the next day to ask what they thought of the affidavit, Greg d'Avignon [a staff member at Campbell's office] said, 'Oh, yeah, we're going through the [CMHC] minutes right now.' Instead of saying, 'Well, you've obviously got a case here, we'll help you.' They used our information to go and search the CMHC minutes for the lease agreement details. They never told us about this," said Miltimore. "They did things like this all the time even though we had always been completely up front with them. On another occasion we had gone through access to information and Campbell's office knew about it right away. They even got copies of letters sent to us before we got them."[30]

By the time the parents made a request to CMHC to look at the minutes of the meetings it was too late. "We got a letter back telling us that the minutes for exactly the six months we were interested in [March to July, 1984] had gone missing. We couldn't believe it."[31]

The parents, now organized into the Granville Island Parents Association, persisted. They held demonstrations on the island and tried to get media attention for their cause. They circulated a petition among island merchants — including merchants in the Kids Only Market — and got a majority to sign. They also stepped up their pressure to get the attention of Campbell. "We wanted Campbell to help us because we knew that she could go to Elmer MacKay [the minister responsible for CMHC], and say, 'Look, let's find out the truth,' " said McPhee. "That's really all we wanted at that point. If the school had to close, fine, we could accept that. But we were determined to get at the truth."

The run-around at Campbell's constituency office continued with avoidance tactics getting more peculiar and crude as the weeks went by. Campbell's head of staff, Diana Lam, refused to talk to the parents at all. The parents dealt instead with Greg d'Avignon. "We said we would really like to talk directly with Ms. Campbell — even by conference call if necessary. He just said she's just too busy. He told us, 'When you talk to me you are talking to Kim Campbell.' He was as arrogant and condescending as she was."[32]

D'Avignon repeatedly misled the parents about where Campbell was and when she would be in town. "One day he told us she wouldn't be here for several weeks and the next day we saw her on TV with Brian Mulroney in Vancouver," said Miltimore.[33] On another occasion, when the parents went to Campbell's office to try to talk with the staff, they locked the door and placed a sign on the window saying they were in a meeting.

Less than a week before the child care centre closed its doors, Campbell's office presented the parents with a proposal. They had identified a space near the island that would be suitable for a new centre. "This was just an obvious ploy to get us off their backs and say they'd done something. It would have meant that we would have to come up with $250,000 on our own and get a matching grant from the province — in eight days? It was not a serious proposal," said Miltimore.[34]

Undeterred by the efforts of Campbell's staff, the parents showed up at a ribbon-cutting ceremony and tried to pass an envelope to Campbell containing documents detailing their concerns and claims. They were stopped by security staff, but not before they got in front of the TV cameras. "She promised, on TV, that she would meet with us the next day. We phoned and phoned and finally got Greg d'Avignon. He just hung up as soon as he realized it was us. We never got the meeting she promised," explains McPhee. "Later, he talked to the media denouncing us as trouble-makers."

The parents then solicited the assistance of a Conservative colleague of Campbell's. "We had an insider working for us, a past president of the Conservatives' Vancouver Centre riding association. He knew Kim Campbell well and he talked to her directly — and even sent her a package of newspaper clippings. He was convinced that her staff were hurting her and told her this — told her that he was worried about her reputation."[35] That effort also got nowhere. The former constituency president ended up so frustrated with Campbell that he began advising the parents. "In the end he was telling us: 'You've got to take this thing to court and do it before Christmas. It's a good time to deal with an issue involving kids.' He was really upset over Campbell's total refusal to respond. It was almost as if he was working against her."[36]

Today, Cherie Miltimore and Janet McPhee remain puzzled by Campbell's stubborn refusal to talk to them or respond to their concerns in any way. "Is this how much she cares about kids?" asks Miltimore. "I'll never understand it. Even politically, it would have been smarter to treat us well and treat kids well. At least she would have shown she cared about the problem even if nothing could be done."[37]

A lot of Tories might readily agree. We are left to speculate as to why Campbell would take such a politically risky course of action — and at the very time that she was planning her leadership campaign. That the media gave the issue sketchy coverage was pure good fortune for Campbell. Risking adverse coverage was poor judgement.

The Over the Rainbow centre had a fair claim that its public subsidy — that is, the reduced rent KOM was obliged to charge — was good use of public money. The use of a building on Granville Island for child care was consistent with the original plan for the island. Campbell, by all normal standards for an MP, should have at the very least met with those concerned to see what could be done to get to the bottom of, if not resolve, the conflict.

Deciphering Campbell's reasoning on this issue is not easy. But she has connections with Granville Island merchants and the island trust's board members that go beyond representing them as their MP. She and her former husband, Nathan Divinsky, were partners in the Bridges Restaurant on the island. While she reportedly sold her share in 1989, she got to know many of the island merchants and she still shows up for openings and other events.

There are other connections. Marilyn Chilvers, one of the Tory appointments to the Granville Island Trust, was a partner with Diana Lam in a public relations firm called Chilvers and Lam. Michael Seelig, another trustee, was a partner with Campbell and Divinsky in the Bridges Restaurant venture. John Pierce, another trustee, recently donated $500 to Campbell's re-election campaign.

Campbell's personal connections aside, as there was no obvious political advantage to Campbell's actions and that of her staff, we may assume that they were driven by her pro-business stance, that it was a simple matter of private property rights winning out over public service. In effect, the termination of the Over the Rainbow child care and pre-school was the privatization of public property. The only people to make an obvious gain were the shareholders of Kids Only Market.

Coming on top of a recently renewed lease for forty-five years, the KOM owners stand to gain a lot of money at public expense. Their annual lease fee to CMHC is $50,000. Their net profit from subletting space to mall merchants is reported to be $360,000. The rent increase demanded of the child care centre was 133 percent — from $3,000 to $7,000 a month — the going commercial rate. That increase in rent revenue alone — $48,000 a year — would virtually pay KOM's annual lease fee.[38]

Kim Campbell, MP: People with AIDS

The treatment accorded the parents of the Over the Rainbow pre-school was part of a pattern in Campbell's Vancouver Centre constituency. The experience of the AIDS community was similar. According to prominent AIDS activist Lauro de Haan, Vancouver Centre has by far the largest number of people with AIDS and HIV of any riding in the country. It took AIDS groups over a year to arrange a meeting with Campbell.

The issue was the federal government's commitment to continue funding AIDS research. The existing five-year commitment of funds was scheduled to end in the spring of 1993 and AIDS groups across the country were getting extremely anxious at the government's silence on any new commitment. Spokespersons wanted something more than five years. AIDS is not a short-term problem and its victims were looking for recognition of that fact. In Vancouver, the voices speaking out were not just those of individuals. Campbell's constituency was home to several of the country's main AIDS organizations.

Lauro de Haan is with the group Vancouver Persons With Aids. "It hit a crescendo last December [1992] when a number of AIDS groups based in Campbell's own riding got together. AIDS Vancouver, the Canadian HIV Trials Network, Persons With Aids and The Positive Women's Network had all been writing to Campbell for at least a year with absolutely no response. We got together and wrote a letter collectively asking if she would consider one meeting with all of us. We still got no response."[39]

De Haan claims dealing with the local constituency office was useless. "If you ever call her constituency office you get the run-around, big-time." But her Ottawa office was scarcely better. "We wrote all sorts of letters. When we talked to them they'd say, 'Oh, we didn't get that letter, we didn't get this letter,' or 'We lost that one.' The lack of action was always chalked up to administrative error — but even so, they never corrected it. None of it was believable. It was her responsibility to approach us anyway. It was quite insulting."[40]

The one time that they were able to put the issue to Campbell was her single meeting with the gay and lesbian community regarding human rights legislation. Campbell, according to de Haan, "sort of lumped us in with the gay community" and invited Mark Mees of the AIDS community to the meeting largely because he was head of the Gay Games. "We used the opportunity to have Mark present Campbell with petitions we had gathered in Vancouver. But nothing came of those, either."

"It's not as if she's never in Vancouver," says de Haan. "She's in the riding a lot but she's just not talking to the affected communities. A lot of it is just ribbon-cutting and photo-op stuff. The reports to her constituents are full of these photo ops and her repeated declarations that she is there, being responsive."[41]

Like the parents from Over the Rainbow child care, AIDS activists tried to get to Campbell through other Tories. "We met with [Vancouver MP and cabinet member] Mary Collins, for example, and expressed to her our frustration — that we couldn't even get to talk to our own MP. I am sure Collins talked to Campbell." Still, the activists got no response. It was not until March 1993, when Campbell's candidacy was a certainty, that she finally met with AIDS groups. The meeting, says de Haan, was "positive in terms of the discussion, but so far nothing new has come of it."[42] By the time of the meeting, AIDS activists knew that the government was renewing funding for the federal AIDS strategy, the main issue that they had wanted to discuss all along.

De Haan and other activists are convinced that Campbell's refusal to meet with them or address the AIDS issue is driven by her efforts to appease her party's right-wing "family caucus" in Parliament. "The family caucus is campaigning hard against any response to AIDS at all. Campbell is a political opportunist and her agenda is to be prime minister. I think that she really does fear them and can't be seen to be close to these issues. She won't stand up to the family caucus."[43]

Vancouver Centre is probably one of the most politically active ridings in the country, with significant sectors of its population displaying a sophisticated political understanding. The other candidates recognize this, says de Haan. "The two women she is running against [the NDP's Betty Baxter, a lesbian, and the Liberal Party's Dr. Hedy Fry] are very responsive and have come to us on their own initiative and asked us to tell them what we need as a community. They have promised to get back to us about how their parties are going to respond to the issues we raise. They are courting the AIDS community."[44]

De Haan believes that Campbell won Vancouver Centre in 1988 by exploiting Pat Carney's popularity and constituency work. "Carney, whatever she believed, was always responsive to our needs. She was vocal on gay rights, on AIDS, on seniors. She would go to bat for us. If there was a problem that could be solved with a phone call to Perrin Beatty or someone else she would do it, no questions asked ... But apparently Campbell has decided that she can't be an activist for her own riding because of its demographics. She has a large gay and lesbian population, a high AIDS and HIV population and a high seniors content — all these are volatile issues because they involve controversy and [government] money or both."[45]

The Business Community

If Campbell was avoiding the AIDS community and the gay and lesbian community, that, at least, was understandable from her need to mollify the family caucus. But for all her pro-business, pro-development stance, and in spite of her status as British Columbia's senior cabinet minister in Mulroney's government, Campbell did not please the business community either. She is widely viewed by business leaders as having done little for the province. Campbell developed a reputation for getting to know Ottawa and the workings of Ottawa quickly and thoroughly — partly as a result of close and intensive coaching by two of the capital's most skilled civil servants, Harry Swain and Fred Drummie. Said Drummie: "We gave her access to much experience — in short how to find her way around."[46] But, says Tex Enemark, that just makes people wonder, "If she's so good, how is it that she has accomplished absolutely nothing for British Columbia?"[47]

By mid-1993, Campbell had failed to bring any major development to Vancouver. She had failed in her own stated goal of making the city a major "communications centre that could compete in Pacific Rim countries with L.A., San Francisco and Seattle."[48] The construction of a Class 8 icebreaker promised for Vancouver shipbuilders was ultimately cancelled despite Campbell's presence on the most important planning committees of cabinet. And even the KAON accelerator for the advanced study of sub-atomic particles, a project Campbell pushed hard, did not go through.

The billion-dollar KAON deal would have been the most expensive science project in Canadian history; Ottawa's contribution was to have been one-third of the cost. It was never enthusiastically endorsed by the science community and was even publicly attacked by Janet Helliwell, the former head of the Science Council of Canada. But the way in which Campbell promoted the project as the senior Tory minister for British Columbia suggested that she was more interested in getting the Socreds re-elected in 1991 than in actually getting KAON off the ground. On September 19, just a few days before the British Columbia election, Campbell announced that Ottawa was committing $236 million to the project. That this was a premature announcement was obvious. Negotiations with the province were not complete and the international funds making up the final third of financing had not been found. In June 1992, after British Columbia demanded more money, the federal cabinet met and secretly decided to withdraw from the project. In short, KAON was dead. This did not stop Campbell from continuing to "promote herself publicly as an avid KAON backer who was fighting to deliver the federal goods to her region."[49]

But Campbell's failure to deliver goes beyond a listing of projects — good and bad — that British Columbia lost. It extends to the partisanship that characterizes her use of power, which disturbs even those who share her pro-business approach. One of her private critics is Tex Enemark, a man well versed in the workings of Ottawa and the exercise of power. An Ottawa lobbyist for several years, Enemark expresses amazement at how Campbell deals with power.

While she was presenting herself as a high-profile promoter of the discredited billion-dollar KAON deal, Campbell ignored an opportunity to help local workers and business people with a project that would have saved 200 jobs. Enemark and some business associates had been approached by the union from the closed-down Wolverine copper tubing plant with a proposal to get the plant operating again. "They presented us with evidence that mismanagement had a role in the plant's demise. We thought it looked promising," said Enemark. He tried to arrange a meeting with Campbell through the local MLA in whose constituency the plant was located, but the MLA could get no co-operation from Campbell's assistants.[50]

On a visit to Ottawa, Enemark decided to use some of his time to ask Campbell to lend a hand in getting the plant revived. He got the same run-around from Campbell's aides that other constituents had experienced. "I tried to talk to people on her staff and I got 'Oh, well, she's terribly busy, you know.' I have been dealing with people in Ottawa for twenty years. And with something like this I just knew that there should have been no trouble, in the space of a week, in finding someone fifteen minutes. To her staffers I said, 'Breakfast, lunch, dinner — whenever — midnight snack, it doesn't matter, I'm free.' "[51] But there was no word from Campbell's office.

Enemark's last Ottawa appointment was in the Prime Minister's office — with none other than Norman Spector, Campbell's old colleague from Bill Bennett's office. "We were chatting after my business was completed and he said what else are you doing in Ottawa and I told him. He said, 'That's really important, you should talk to Kim Campbell.' I explained to him what I had gone through and he acted immediately — called up Ray Castelli [Campbell's chief of staff]. Even he had trouble getting to Castelli but finally did manage to get me fifteen minutes with him. I told Spector that I was really tight for time as I was going to catch a plane. Norman waved his hand and said, 'My limousine will take you to the Justice Department, go and pick up your bags from your hotel, come back, pick you up and take you to the airport.' "[52]

Enemark still shakes his head at Campbell's behaviour and her apparent lack of interest in trying to save 200 jobs in her own province. "There is, irrespective of politics and partisan considerations, a kind of working together to get things done that are in the common interest. But beyond that there is also a basis of civility in the way you treat people. Now Norman and I have had, over the years, more than our share of knock-down, drag-out differences of opinion but he understood the importance of working together in a civilized manner. But she has a very peculiar idea about power, about government and about what we are all trying to accomplish in society."[53]

It is understandable that Campbell might not be eager to co-operate with a former Liberal politician with whom she did fierce battle in an emotional and bitter campaign. Yet the same could be said for Norman Spector, a Tory whose partisan credentials go back two decades. Campbell allowed her partisan feelings and loyalty to override her responsibility to her own constituency.

These are a few of the many incidents known to Campbell's constituents and other Vancouver residents. The gay and lesbian community has felt not just excluded but betrayed by Campbell for her amendments to the human rights legislation and because she has given them almost no access to her to discuss their concerns. "After eight years of [government] promises Kim Campbell introduced legislation that didn't go as far as the courts — an act which institutionalizes discrimination," says Betty Baxter, the NDP candidate running against Campbell.[54] Activists in Campbell's own riding took the initiative in calling for the withdrawal of her human rights amendments regarding gays and lesbians.

Seniors — who have their own complaints about Campbell's lack of concern — gays and lesbians, people with AIDS, women needing child care, business people and unionists wanting help to create jobs: these people represent the key demographic constituencies of Vancouver Centre, where Campbell will have to get re-elected.

Campbell's leadership race was characterized by her promise of a new way of doing politics: the politics of inclusion. When asked what distinguished her from Brian Mulroney, she replied, "Fundamentally, I am a democrat."[55] But we judge people by what they do and not what they say — whether they are politicians, friends or anyone else we encounter. Campbell has been in politics long enough for us to judge her actions and thereby assess what she says to see if it rings true.

Campbell should be judged not by what she promises to do in the future but by what she has already done in the job that is supposed to prepare her for being prime minister. Her behaviour as a candidate and an MP suggests that she will be one of the least accessible and responsive prime ministers we have had.

Minister of Justice

Kim Campbell is a professional politician and has made hundreds of speeches. But of these, two stand out, in part because they so dramatically demonstrate a theme that winds through her political career: the contrast between what she says and what she does. Whether this contrast indicates political expediency or just the gap between promise and reality is an important question. If we are to look to Campbell's record to tell us the answer, then her record in Justice is probably the best place to look. The rest of her political career is fairly short. The federal Justice portfolio was not only her most influential political position, but it was also the one that she held longer than any other, except for school trustee. Campbell was Minister of Justice from 1990 to 1993. Justice proved to be a portfolio that meshed perfectly with her greatest political passion: the rule of law.

The first of these key speeches was made in Vancouver on June 11, 1991 at Women, Law and the Administration of Justice, a symposium that Campbell initiated. It was a meeting filled with promise; never before had those who were demanding changes in the law and in the way it worked been in a room together with those who had the power and the authority to implement the changes. It was a classic example of what Campbell has called "inclusive politics."

The second speech was made in Ottawa on April 14, 1992, on the occasion of the tenth anniversary of the Charter of Rights and Freedoms, perhaps the most lasting legacy of Pierre Trudeau. Campbell used the occasion to rail against the Supreme Court, suggesting that it was usurping the role of Parliament. Many were surprised: the speech seemed to reveal a fundamental hostility towards the notion of legislated rights. It was not lost on those women who were fighting for equality that this justice minister was very different from the one who had spoken almost a year earlier. It is in the political distance between these speeches that Campbell's record lies.

Women, Law and Justice

Campbell's decision to organize the 1991 Vancouver symposium came after two lacklustre years in cabinet. Her first portfolio was the junior post of Secretary of State for Indian Affairs. She attracted some attention when she presided over major cuts to post-secondary education for Indians and when she steadfastly refused to consider a separate justice system for aboriginal people, something that several provincial jurisdictions were considering and which virtually all aboriginal organizations had called for. She took credit for getting British Columbia started on the road to comprehensive land claims, although this was something the province had been considering for some time. The Vancouver symposium, a year into her Justice mandate, may have been designed by Campbell to increase her profile, particularly on issues which could set her apart from other Tories.

Hopes were high at the Vancouver symposium. Rosalie Abella, one of the country's foremost feminist legal authorities and chair of the Ontario Law Reform Commission, saw the promise of the three-day meeting as a journey down the yellow brick road. "I see the feisty Dorothy leading the public, politicians, and the legal professionals to find the Wizard of Ms to provide the heart, courage and brains and a way back to a kind of Kansas where everyone is safe and protected and cared for."[1] It was a compelling image. Although Abella and the other feminists among the 250 delegates had no illusions about the difficulty that changing decades of sexism in the legal system would entail, the symposium was seen as an enormous step forward. They had fought for over a decade just to have someone in authority acknowledge that there was sexism in the system. And that much they got.

Campbell's words held great promise for the participants — both in terms of recognizing the barriers to change and in her apparent willingness to challenge them. "Perhaps it's a little bit disquieting — it's so new and different. For those who make change, we're not always used to being nose-to-nose with those who want us to exercise our powers in a certain way. And for those who have for so long been knocking at the door it can be sometimes a little disconcerting when the door is open and they're allowed to sit down and state their views."[2]

This was heady stuff and implied that Campbell saw herself as among friends with common goals. "Every once in a while, justice has to lift up her blindfold and take a gander ... to understand the human reality and the complexity before her. Perhaps women really do have a very different way of looking at justice."[3]

For Campbell, the symposium was a real exercise in risk-taking: she must have known that living up to any of the promises made to the progressive feminists was going to be extremely difficult, given the Tory cabinet and caucus. But more important, particularly given her later incarnation as a leadership candidate, she must have known that bringing together dozens of critics of the legal system was a dramatic way to open the door to an enormous amount of criticism. In addition, these critics knew and could demonstrate that the majority of Canadians supported them in most, if not all, of the kinds of changes they were seeking. Inclusiveness in this context meant that Campbell acknowledged that if it was a government's business to create legislation to respond to changes in the political culture, it was these women in the room with her, invited by her, who were the voice of those changes.

Women's groups had identified many legal and human rights issues, and each was represented by one or more organizations and by many individual activists and academics. The issue of male violence against women was high on the agenda. Lee Lakeman of the Canadian Association of Sexual Assault Centres, like the other women at the Vancouver meeting, was not about to be swayed by the mere image of change. "There is a basic contradiction between the Conservative politic and a feminist politic. The onus is on the Conservatives. What is overwhelmingly clear is that the women of Canada overwhelmingly support the feminists on these questions. The Conservatives will have to prove that they can unite with us, not the other way around."[4]

Campbell asked for recommendations and probably got a lot more than she bargained for. The women at the symposium were not just talking about legislation or administration; they were demanding structural changes that would deal with the fundamentals of women's position in society. An organizer for a women's shelter said, "We don't want to see women of poverty put in prison because they can't afford to pay the rent or they can't afford to feed their children."[5] Others attacked the government for its constant erosion of grants to their advocacy organizations, pointing out that the symposium's $350,000 budget for three days was larger than the annual grant to the National Action Committee on the Status of Women (NAC). Jean Swanson, vice-president of the

National Anti-Poverty Organization, answered Campbell's challenge for recommendations with these: "The welfare laws, the minimum wage laws and taxation laws must be changed if there is to be progress."[6]

Campbell raised expectations with the language she used and with her call for "not just talk" but concrete recommendations. "I have felt, since I was made Minister of Justice, the clock ticking. There is no question that sexism, racism and other forms of discrimination are clearly systemic problems in the justice system... And the passion here results from the discrepancy between what is seen in the law and the reality of people's lives."[7] Here, and again later, Campbell seemed to allude to questions of social class: "For the large part, the law deals with assumptions that are only realities for a small portion of Canadians."[8]

Her call for concrete suggestions brought forward literally hundreds of recommendations, ranging from changes in legislation, to changes in legal procedures, to measures to address widespread social attitudes towards women. It is unclear just what Campbell expected to do with all these recommendations. She had been in her position as minister for over a year and she certainly knew her cabinet and caucus colleagues well enough to know that she would never get dozens of these recommendations by them, even if she agreed with them herself.

And many she did not agree with. She simply refused to support a separate justice system for native people, for example, despite virtually unanimous backing for the idea from women's organizations. She rejected a quota for the appointment of women judges. But on the issue of violence against women and reforming judicial attitudes towards women, Campbell did make commitments. She agreed to address gender bias in the system and to take the recommendations she had received into account.

Many at the symposium gave her high marks for the risks she was taking and the seeming empathy with which she responded to three days of brutal attacks on the justice system. Roz Currie, from the National Association of Women and the Law, put her scepticism aside and said that it seemed, at least, that "Campbell *cared*."[9]

But they were in no mood for being suckered, either. Said Currie, "I'll have to wait and see if she implements our recommendations before I decide whether she has built any bridges to the women's movement."[10] Shelagh Day, human rights activist and vice-president of NAC, probably summed up the feminist perspective of the symposium best: "From the women's perspective the justice system is in crisis. The symposium has been an excellent opportunity ... to talk openly about the problem. We've worked very hard during this conference and now we're looking for action."[11] The sense of accomplishment was symbolized by the "hugs and tears" of the participants as the conference ended. If Campbell let them down, Canada's feminist community would not likely be willing to suspend their scepticism so easily again.

If Campbell was daunted by the expectations she had raised in the minds of many in the women's movement, she did not show it a few weeks later when Charlotte Gray interviewed her for an article in *Saturday Night*. "Sitting in her Ottawa office ... Campbell grins as she recalls the adrenaline [the symposium] generated. She speaks with the ingenuous glee of a lawyer after a court victory, rather than the caution of a battle-scarred forty-four year old whose ambitions and prospects are the subject of much speculation."[12] Gray does not pose the question that her observation about victory implies. If Campbell won, who lost?

Throughout her campaign for the leadership of the Conservative Party during the spring of 1993, Campbell tried to appeal to people by the repeated declaration that she was committed to the "politics of inclusion." The Vancouver symposium, presumably, was just that: an invitation to citizens to participate directly in the political process; to influence social change by influencing Parliament, the institution that actually implemented social change through legislation, regulation and the allocation of resources. But in fact, a year after Vancouver, little had been accomplished. The vacuum of policy initiatives that women's representatives had been decrying for ten or fifteen years was still unfilled. Even in areas where women had highest hopes for Campbell, the system was actually going backwards. By October 1991, the proportion of women on the bench had actually fallen.[13] Women's groups still found it necessary to pressure the Mulroney government on the whole broad range of issues affecting women.

It was not just the government that women were pursuing in the name of equality and social justice. It was the courts, too. If Campbell would not or could not make the changes that women — and society in general — wanted, then perhaps the courts would. And that is where Campbell's other key speech reveals her fundamentally conservative politics.

The Charter Speech

This speech, delivered on the tenth anniversary of the proclamation of the Charter, was Campbell's political and philosophical response to its use by those individuals and groups seeking equality in Canadian society. Since its proclamation, the courts have been remarkably responsive to this use of the Charter, far more responsive and progressive in recent years than the most optimistic observers had predicted. Of course, those who worried openly about the courts undermining the supremacy of Parliament were saying "I told you so."

The Supreme Court and some of the lower courts had been effecting political changes of historic importance to equality-seeking groups who had been stonewalled for years by federal governments. The Supreme Court had struck down the abortion law on the grounds that it violated the Charter. The Ontario Court of Appeal had ruled that the Canadian Human Rights Act violated the Charter by failing to protect gays and lesbians from discrimination. The courts had intervened on behalf of the disabled in the area of accommodation. The judiciary was proving to be a bold and imaginative player not only in narrow matters of "the law," but in matters affecting and reflecting the political culture and social values.

Campbell's speech on the occasion of the Charter's anniversary makes for remarkable reading. Her key point was the complaint that the courts are usurping Parliament's role in Canadian society. She started by telling her audience that "we are *celebrating* the tenth anniversary of the charter,"[14] but soon her speech turned into a litany of admonishments, warnings and veiled threats against the judiciary for their involvement in the political process, many of them delivered ad lib. Warning that we are becoming more American in our approach, she stated, "We, too, [like the Americans] have become an increasingly litigious and confrontational society, and I fear that some of our citizens have begun to look to courts — rather than to Parliament and legislatures — as agents of political and social change."[15]

Nowhere in this speech was there any indication that she had participated in the 1991 Vancouver symposium or listened to the scores of women who were giving her one loud message: Parliament and legislatures were denying the political and social change that the vast majority of women had been demanding for over a decade. There was not a hint in her talk that she was aware that women and others were going to the courts precisely because the institutions that had traditionally redressed grievances had slammed the door. The world that Campbell lived in when she wrote this speech did not seem to be the same one she inhabited when she told the Vancouver symposium that she heard the "clock ticking," emphasizing the urgency for change. She now warned, "We must not lose our ability to search for consensus and compromise."

As a minister with a seat on the priorities and planning committee of Brian Mulroney's cabinet, Campbell was a key player in the design of all Tory policies and the methods by which they were implemented. Just four months earlier, the government had forced the GST through Parliament by way of eighteen patronage appointments to the Senate. Yet in her attack on the courts, she argued, "We must ensure that Canadians do not come to believe that public policy issues can only be resolved by a court decision. In particular, it is our duty to ensure that our political processes remain effective agents of social change, and that Canadians have confidence in the ability of those processes to advance the larger good."[16]

The glaring contradiction between the reality of the Tory government's policies and Campbell's lament about the activist courts can best be understood in the light of her political philosophy. It is here that Campbell is most clearly revealed as very conservative, in the traditional sense of that word. Campbell often refers in interviews to her favourite philosopher, Edmund Burke, and even in her speech about the Charter she broke from her prepared text to lecture the audience about the supremacy of Parliament.

Ken Norman, a Saskatoon law professor, heard Campbell's speech. An authority on human rights, Norman was, at the time, a member of the Equality Rights Panel of the Court Challenges Program, an agency devoted to helping people use the Charter to address issues of discrimination. "Toward the end of her speech she referred to Edmund Burke, saying, 'You know, I've thought about this and Burke was right. He said that the law as authored by Parliament is to be seen as one would see the directions given by a loving parent and if it is flawed this is no reason to celebrate, it is a cause to grieve.' In other words, if the parent makes a bad rule we should just go along with it because it was made with good intentions and we should respect our parents."[17]

The Burkean view of democracy sees Parliament as supreme — not just in the sense that it is elected by the people but in the more restricted sense that, once elected, it can by definition do no wrong. It is this view of Parliament that makes conservative parliamentarians so nervous about the concept of rights that come before the laws they pass, but that they cannot touch.

Anything that challenges duly elected government is treated with suspicion by those adhering to Burkean views. "Challenges to government are not to be encouraged," says Norman, analyzing Campbell's speech and the attitude it reveals. "Government is to be seen as benevolent and must be respected. In effect the Burkean elevates the given over the ideal because at least the given is something we know, and there isn't blood in the streets and heads being chopped off with the guillotine. Anything that is visionary or utopian, anything that is looking for a different world, a different kind of social order, is very disturbing to a social conservative."[18]

It was from this perspective that Campbell attacked the Supreme Court in her Charter speech for striking down a B.C. law that decreed a mandatory jail sentence for anyone found driving while impaired. Norman comments, "She took the court to task for having the effrontery to change that social norm. Whose business is it to do that? It is Parliament's."[19]

What has Campbell and other philosophical conservatives alarmed is that the Supreme Court has made positive rulings on rights cases. That is, it has not restricted itself to simply striking down laws which it finds in violation of the Charter. It effectively creates new laws which — in equality cases, for example — give positive entitlement to individuals.

The most significant equality case, because of the precedent it set, was the first Supreme Court of Canada judgement on the Charter. (Though the Charter was proclaimed in 1982, there was a three-year moratorium before the equality rights section came into effect.) The *Andrews* case, which came down in February 1989, established principles for understanding what equality meant that had enormous implications for later cases. Judge Bertha Wilson declared that the Charter's equality section was designed to "protect those groups who suffer social, political and legal disadvantage... " Ken Norman explains, "This established that equality was not just an empty idea but a substantive one. It requires that one look into the question of who is advantaged and who is disadvantaged: Is this plaintiff a member of a group that is historically disadvantaged socially, politically or economically? Only if the answer to this question is 'yes' does this person have standing in the court to raise an equality question."[20] This case eliminated the early trend in Charter cases — and cases brought under the earlier Bill of Rights — that saw men challenging laws against statutory rape by arguing that they discriminated against men.

The *Andrews* case also established the notion of remedy: those discriminated against must have their situation remedied in a positive manner. It was the action of the courts on this principle that had Campbell so agitated at the Charter anniversary conference. She was particularly exercised over what is called "the doctrine of extension," in which the court in effect implements its own decisions. The classic example was the *Schacter* case in which Shalom Schacter, a natural parent, demanded the same parental benefits that were available to an adoptive parent. Rather than just declare the law in violation of the equality provisions, the court "extended" the law's benefits to Schacter. In similar, earlier cases where benefits were not extended, governments in British Columbia and Saskatchewan simply changed violating welfare programs to deny certain benefits to all concerned, thus eliminating discrimination by depriving an even larger group in addition to those already deprived and seeking equality.

But more important, the *Andrews* case, and others based on it, injected into the courts issues of social class and oppression. In effect, these cases invited into the courts the kind of struggles between élites and the disadvantaged that Conservatives claim do not exist.

Burke versus Voltaire = Campbell versus Trudeau?

Edmund Burke's view of rights provides insight into Campbell's position: he claimed that the idea of equality was "a monstrous fiction." He advised legislators to place their own thoughts ahead of their constituents', because he did not trust the "rabble" to dictate to governments what they should do, in an outpouring of populist sentiment. This helps us understand that Campbell supported the GST not just because she was in the cabinet, but because she fundamentally believes in majoritarian rule: that is, the conviction that it is in recognizing the interests of the majority that governments promote stability and consensus. In this view of society, it is the tyranny of the minority that represents the greatest threat and that accounts for the conservative's identification of groups advocating for women, aboriginal people, the poor and the disabled as "interest groups." When Brian Mulroney forced through the GST, he said, "When faced with choosing what is popular or what is good for the country, I always choose what is good for the country." Campbell would have been nodding with approval.

There is no question that Pierre Trudeau's creation of the Charter of Rights and Freedoms was a fundamental departure from the parliamentary tradition based on Britain's Westminster model. Trudeau's intellectual roots are in the Enlightenment and Voltaire, while Campbell finds herself in the camp of Edmund Burke. While Voltaire elevated reason above all else, Burke denied it a pre-eminent place in society. Ordinary people were not equipped to use reason.

This notion has been most clearly expressed by Campbell in her reflections on the defeat of the Charlottetown accord. She told an audience at Harvard University that it was the "civically competent" citizens in Canada who voted Yes on the referendum. In spite of the fact that polls indicated that 70 percent of Canadians made the effort to read at least part of the accord, Campbell told her Harvard audience that they did not understand what they read. "They simply cannot relate to what it means to allow a provincial government to do something as opposed to the federal government ... [or understand] devolution of powers to aboriginal communities ..." Those who voted Yes were more educated, "The 'yes' side had a very, very preponderant representation of people who have responsibility for decision making. [These] were people who played elite roles ... positions of responsibility in Canadian society. [Their vote] reflected the attitudes of people who had a specific competence."[21] In short, the people who voted No simply did not understand what they were doing. They were not competent to decide and so made the wrong decision.

Looking at the world through Campbell's Burkean eyes, we see that the aloofness and snobbishness that she often reveals are not simply bad habits or personality traits. They reflect her view of the world and her understanding of how politics should be carried out. The proper way to run a society is to hand over the task to the educated élites, those with "civic competence."

Campbell's attitude to the Charter and to human rights in general, and her actions in dealing with these as Justice Minister, reveal a determination to turn back the clock in the area of rights and to re-establish both majoritarian democracy and the supremacy of Parliament. We may never know whether or not she was given the Justice portfolio by Mulroney in order to do just this. But there is no question that she is far more dedicated to the task than her boss ever was.

In these areas, more than in any others, Campbell demonstrates how ideologically driven she is. For she is attempting to turn back ten years of Canadian cultural change. According to Ken Norman, "The idea of Canada engaged in continual, existential angst as we try to rediscover who we are, as we become more multi-racial, and our differences are heightened and we become more regional and more strident in our pluralism — this idea is highly disturbing to Kim Campbell, the social conservative. She wants to engage in practical compromises over minority rights in order to achieve what? Not the actualization of any of the values of the minorities but in order to achieve social stability — that's her objective."[22] This perception of the rightful role of government is fundamentally hostile to the Supreme Court's explicit interpretation of the meaning of equality in the Charter: that it means "recognizing and accommodating difference."

Imposing a rigid notion of social cohesion on a country as increasingly diverse as Canada would be extremely difficult. In this determined objective, Campbell is much more akin to Preston Manning and Reform Party guru William Gairdner than she is to Brian Mulroney. Both are so ideologically committed to taking us back to a calmer, more stable time that they are willing to impose ideas that have been left behind by the "human reality" that Campbell frequently refers to as a factor in her political principles. "It is a vision which I think makes a bad fit with a pluralistic, federal state such as ours," says Norman. "It is almost unimaginable to me that someone can talk about that kind of social cohesion in a country like Canada. It was hard enough even in a country like Britain two hundred years ago — a unitary, almost homogeneous culture ethnically, compared to ours."[23]

For better or worse, not only Canada but the world in general has seen an increasing emphasis on the idea of rights. Since 1946 and the formation of the United Nations, the notion of entitlement has been encouraged by a series of covenants, treaties and declarations and has been supported by UN agencies. The focus in all of this is the plight of the human being and the problem of tyranny. The most effective response to tyranny has been seen to be the declaration of respect for human rights. In Canada, women, aboriginal people and others talk about historical entitlement and collective rights. It is this trend that Campbell seems determined to resist. Says Ken Norman, "I see Kim Campbell rather like Canute on his throne ordering the tide to stay away."[24]

When Campbell rails against the courts for usurping the role of Parliament, it is not just the courts' "political" interventions she objects to. She resists the whole notion of demands by marginalized groups for changes in the social structure and political culture. This was made clear in her speech at Harvard in which she attacked groups using the Charter. Since the Charter came into effect, said Campbell, "we had the unleashing of what has come to be called Charter groups, groups that assert rights based on the newly defined rights in the Charter ... These groups have developed into interest groups ... [which] define themselves as grievance groups which is a negative thing. There is no such thing as an unmixed blessing. One of the aspects of the political dynamic that was unleashed in '82 was the appearance ... of a whole variety of groups competing for the benefits of governments."[25] Campbell can barely disguise her hostility towards advocacy groups, twice using the term "unleashed."

Trudeau did more than introduce the Charter of Rights and Freedoms into Canadian politics. In the early seventies, his government responded to broad-based social movements by implementing policies that reflected the principle of "participatory democracy." Hundreds of citizens' advocacy groups received government funding to put forward their grievances and their claims on government and society. In effect, Trudeau's government — and provincial governments which followed suit — institutionalized the kind of continuous political activism that Burke and conservatives in general abhor. The prominence of advocacy groups in Canadian politics is, for Campbell, the antithesis of the politics of stewardship and the social cohesion it is supposed to bring. This may explain why she was so willing to throw political advantage to the winds by ignoring the AIDS community and the child care advocates in her own riding of Vancouver Centre. And it is almost certainly what prompted her to include in her campaign for leadership the promise that she would demand of advocacy groups that they publicly register the favours they are asking of government.

Killing the Court Challenges Program

If there was a single focal point for the conflict of visions between women's groups and Campbell, it was the Court Challenges Program (CPP), which operated from 1985–1992. With a modest budget of $2.7 million in the final year of its existence, the CCP was the manifestation of the notion that ordinary citizens have the right to challenge the status quo and to have their day in court. Although it began as a federal program to fund challenges under the language provision of the Charter, women's groups were successful in having it expanded to cover a much broader range of equality issues raised by the Charter.

The program was based on a simple and obvious premise: litigation — that is, access to the courts — was normally available only to people who had enormous wealth. If Charter rights, which are realized and enforced through litigation, were to be taken seriously, this inequality had to be recognized and remedied. The Court Challenges Program was intended to redress the balance between those who had and those who lacked the resources needed to bring their grievances to court.

Given its modest budget, the CCP was remarkably successful. It was originally a joint responsibility of the Justice Department and the Department of the Secretary of State. Gradually, it came under the Secretary of State alone, not simply to emphasize its arms-length relationship with government but because the Secretary of State was the department of government that "celebrated our differences and where political dissent is encouraged."[26] Justice still took an active interest and had some authority over its activities.

In spite of unanimous recommendations of a parliamentary committee to continue funding it, the Court Challenges Program was cancelled in early 1992. No amount of lobbying on its behalf by the legal profession, politicians of all stripes, editorialists or the groups affected had any impact. There had been virtually no negative press, no group was complaining about the program or even mentioning it — with the single exception of the Reform Party. But Campbell had wanted the program dead for a long time. And once it was killed nothing was going to revive it.

It was ideology that killed the program. The elimination of the CCP was a small but effective step in limiting the access of marginalized groups to the courts and to the rights guaranteed in the Charter. A brief examination of some of the challenges that did make it through the system explains why Campbell wanted the program out of the way. The aggressive manner in which her department dealt with successful challenges and the efforts to limit the victories that they produced for women, gays, lesbians and others reinforce the view that the Justice Department was much more committed to the status quo than to justice.

Part of the CCP's pro-active approach to equality issues was to establish a panel that examined cases with the explicit purpose of funding those that advanced equality for disadvantaged groups. In 1989, they held workshops and meetings across the country, culminating in a national meeting of equality-seeking groups in Ottawa, where representatives of sixty groups shared their experiences and learned about seeking equality under the Charter.

Court Challenges staff and the lawyers who took advocacy cases discovered that Justice was becoming increasingly aggressive in its approach — not simply trying to win cases, but doing everything possible to prevent the courts from making decisions. Kathleen Ruff, who was the director of the Court Challenges Program after 1988, still gets angry when she recalls the Justice Department's approach. "There was a whole number of cases where they used every tactic in the book to delay a decision or make it more expensive for the plaintiff. One case involving the Science Council of Canada was just obvious and blatant racism, yet they fought it tooth and nail. Even when they agreed that a case showed discrimination they fought it. Their approach, as far I was concerned, was really immoral."[27]

The CCP typically allotted $35,000 for a case, but time and again this turned out to be inadequate. "We were forever getting stories back from lawyers — who had to make reports justifying their billings — saying 'You have to know that I've been fighting all sorts of examinations for discovery, interlocutory motions, procedural delays. I've already spent $39,000 and we haven't even gotten to trial yet.' They and we just hadn't anticipated all the roadblocks."[28]

Justice also used its power to demand information on the cases that Court Challenges was funding — a demand the program felt obliged to meet. Ken Norman, a four-year member of the CCP panel that decided which cases would be funded, sees two motives behind this interference: "One, to have better data for the case they were going to have to fight. But equally important, to compile a record of sins of commission — to build a case to eliminate the program. 'Look at what they've done — they've funded the Innu of Labrador to challenge the military.'"[29]

This interference by the Justice Department pre-dated Campbell, but continued and even expanded under her tenure, according to Ruff. "One of the cases under Campbell's reign involved discrimination against an immigrant family denied status because they had a disabled child. We worked for months preparing the case and of course the point was not just to help the plaintiff but to strike down the offending regulation. Just as we were to go to court they settled with the plaintiff."[30] It was, says Ruff, a deliberate strategy from the beginning to drain the CCP budget, use up as much time as possible and, most important, to keep discriminatory regulations in place by denying the opportunity to set a legal precedent in court.

The Canadian Council of Churches was one victim of these unethical stonewalling tactics. The Council was challenging a section of the new Immigration Act that pertained to refugees. The Department launched an action challenging the standing of the Council in the case. "In effect," says Norman, "the department was saying, 'These people [the Council of Churches] are busybodies and the court should strike down this action without even looking at its merits. The only people who should have standing are the immigrants who land at Mirabel and who are put back on the plane because we think they are bogus refugees.' Now, of course, these people are only in the country for a few hours before they are put on a plane and sent back to Yugoslavia or wherever. This was typical of the cynical attitude of the Department of Justice."[31]

Ruff was clearly disgusted with Campbell's approach. " 'Let the democratic process work,' says Campbell. But Justice would never, ever say to us, 'We'll sit down and consult with you to see if there is an issue.' Instead it was, 'Just don't you dare use the courts to force us to change the law or we'll smash your face.' "[32]

A group of sexual orientation cases most clearly demonstrated Campbell's particular determination to limit the courts' effectiveness and rein in the notion of rights. "At first I didn't know if she had any hand in these cases at all," said Ken Norman. "But we funded four sexual orientation cases involving the RCMP and the military. In the end there was never a trial in any of these cases. Justice would take every possible step they could to delay, to run up the cost ... to Court Challenges and at the last moment settle in order to keep the courts from taking hold of the helm. At that point it seemed to me that Campbell's hand was in it because she was trying in her own caucus to deal with the issue."[33]

When a gay prisoner petitioned the courts for equal conjugal visiting rights, Justice first argued that the matter was not covered by the Charter. When Justice lost in federal court, it appealed and changed its position, now holding that the Charter did protect the right of the man in question to conjugal visits — but only with a woman.

Campbell had inherited the issue from her predecessors, including John Crosbie who, in 1986, had committed the government to changing the Human Rights Act to include sexual orientation, following the unanimous recommendation of a parliamentary committee. But Tory MPs in the "family caucus" were having none of it. True to her views on the supremacy of Parliament, if Campbell could not get the amendment past the caucus, she was determined not to allow the courts to usurp the legislators' role.

Nonetheless, the legal and human rights case for including sexual orientation in the Act was overwhelming. The Ontario Court of Appeal ruled in 1992 that the Canadian Human Rights Act violated the Charter of Rights. At that point, Campbell seemed to give up the fight. She immediately announced that there was no need to amend the Act because the decision had the same effect.

But Campbell soon changed her mind. She introduced amendments to the Act that purported to respond to the Ontario Court of Appeal decision but were in fact aimed at restricting the impact of the decision. The amendments added sexual orientation to the Act, but also defined the meaning of "family" as strictly heterosexual. One of the key objectives of the gay and lesbian community in their equality challenges was to establish the right to receive the employee spousal benefits available to heterosexual couples. That objective was implied in the Ontario court decision and would very likely have been granted in subsequent challenges. Campbell's move to restrict the meaning of the decision was widely condemned by gay and lesbian activists as well as human rights activists.

"I think this recommendation, made just before Campbell left Justice, is quite shameful. It is worse than doing nothing about the act," says Norman. "The Charter is about respecting difference. What we as the dominant culture are saying [with this amendment] is that we *officially* disapprove of the way some people live. We're going to say, in the law, to lesbian women choosing to live together, that you are disapproved. You have hurt no one and there is no harm in what you are doing but we will use the law to say, 'You are not a couple.' "[34]

Campbell's assault on the Charter has been effective. Without the Court Challenges Program, disadvantaged groups have little access to the courts. The program's moderate budget represents the difference between a Charter that is a meaningful instrument in carrying out its intended and now-established purpose and one that is virtually meaningless. Poor people in particular will be at the mercy of governments.

Ken Norman cites two cases illustrating the future under a Campbell government. The first is the *Mossop* case in which a gay man was denied permission by his government employer to take a day of bereavement leave to attend the funeral of his partner's father. Bereavement leave was available to different-sex partners, but the employer refused to accept the man's male partner as a spouse. The court ruled on behalf of the Justice Department in February 1993, holding that the denial was not a violation of the equality section of the Charter. "That," says Norman, "is simply outrageous. And it shows that Campbell as a social conservative is willing to do something completely unprincipled to impose her narrow view of social cohesion."

The second is the *Finlay* case, also decided by the Supreme Court in early 1993. James Finlay from Manitoba argued before the Supreme Court that the Manitoba government was violating the Canada Assistance Plan (CAP) by deducting a portion of his welfare cheque each month. The province was cutting Finlay's allowance to recover overpayments resulting from a bureaucratic error for which Finlay shared no responsibility. When the CAP, which provides funding to provincial welfare programs, was announced by an earlier Liberal government, its intent was to meet basic needs. Finlay's argument was that welfare rates in Manitoba just met basic needs, and that any deduction from those rates violated the CAP.

The Supreme Court ruled against Finlay, saying, in effect, that it had no responsibility to police the bilateral arrangement between the federal government and Manitoba, regardless of whether the Manitoba action violated the intent of the legislation. This very recent case is the wave of the future in the eyes of many rights activists.

The *Finlay* case is in many ways a product of Campbell's Department of Justice, which oversaw the alteration of the Supreme Court itself. *Finlay* was decided on a five-to-four vote. The deciding vote belonged to Jack Major, the most recent appointee to the Supreme Court and one strongly influenced by Campbell, according to Norman. "Right after Major was appointed, he made a very revealing statement regarding his social conservative leanings and how he intended to deal with Charter challenges. He said, 'If a person wants to make changes in this country, he ought to get himself elected.' That displays a thoroughgoing misunderstanding of what it means to have an entrenched Charter of Rights in this country."[35]

If there was any doubt that Campbell harboured an intense hostility towards the Court Challenges Program and its pro-active stance on equality rights, it was dramatically dispelled at a meeting on February 27, 1993 in Ottawa between Campbell and human rights activists from across the country. Called to discuss proposed amendments to the Human Rights Act, the meeting coincided, ironically, with the government's surprise announcement that it was cancelling the program.

The relationship between human rights and the CCP was so critical that an adverse response to the decision at the meeting was inevitable. Campbell's reaction to the criticism revealed her hostility towards the program and the court's interpretation of the Charter. Later, in the House and Commons and in letters to supporters of the Program, Campbell would studiously avoid any responsibility for the CCP, referring all queries to the Department of Secretary of State. But at the meeting, Campbell aggressively defended the decision to cancel the program, reinforcing the strong suspicion of those present that she, as the senior minister of the two who shared responsibility for the program, was behind the decision. Ruff attended the meeting and recalled Campbell simply attacking all those who raised objections. "She characterized our comments as 'misguided, foolish and perverse.' "[36] Shelagh Day was appalled. "Campbell was so vigorous in her defence of the cancellation of the program and so condescending, so disrespectful of all these concerned people that it was extremely offensive."[37]

In the aftermath of the decision, a huge lobbying effort was undertaken, with some very influential people joining in to urge the Justice Minister to use her influence to have the decision reversed. Those writing to Campbell included the deans of several law schools, the presidents of the Canadian Bar Association and several provincial bar associations, many lawyers and others in the justice field, and even Bertha Wilson, the retired Supreme Court justice. Wilson informed Campbell that she and the other justices on the Supreme Court had seen "what an invaluable contribution this program made." All the petitions had essentially the same message: this was a matter of access to justice. They were asking her as minister to fight for justice.

Campbell's response was the reverse of her spirited and detailed defence of the decision at the meeting of human rights activists. She denied any responsibility or even any interest in the program or its demise. She informed the senior figures in the legal community who petitioned her that she would pass their letters on to Gerry Weiner, the Minister for the Secretary of State. When questioned on the program in the House of Commons, Campbell refused to answer, handing the questions over to Weiner — who seemed confused about why the decision had been made. Arguing a line that was beyond his department's competence to determine, Weiner claimed there was a solid base of jurisprudence to protect the rights of the disadvantaged, and so the program was not needed. The cases which had been determined by the courts provided all the precedents necessary to protect those facing discrimination. "I guess that is why we acted as we did," said Weiner.[38]

Did Campbell herself cancel the Court Challenges Program? There is no way of knowing, but some in human rights circles think it was more likely the family caucus. Pat File, who worked for the CCP, takes this position. "It was the family caucus ... and some Western MPs who were very upset about the gay and lesbian cases. They saw [the CCP] as a program that was funding sexual orientation as an issue and there was a [false] perception that we also funded abortion cases. Our impression is that it was [Deputy Prime Minister and Finance Minister Don] Mazankowski and those around him who really made the decision. It was an effort to appease those [Tories] who had gone over to the Reform party."[39] That impression was reinforced by a letter from Mazankowski to the Minority Advocacy and Rights Council: "The objective of the program was to clarify aspects of the Charter and not to provide perpetual access to federal finances or development resources to advocacy groups."[40]

While the government was cutting the $2.7 million from the CCP, it was increasing Campbell's budget for litigation by $16 million, leaving little doubt about the department's intention of fighting any future challenges. When challenged about the increase in her budget in the House of Commons, Campbell stated, "The reason for the increases ... was because of costly legal challenges under the Charter of Rights and Freedoms that the government is obliged to defend."[41] Those challenges would now be few and far between. And while Campbell may not have had a direct hand in killing the CCP, she was obviously relieved to see it die.

Chipping Away at Human Rights

The Court Challenges Program was not the only irritant in Campbell's Burkean world. The parallel institutions to the Charter of Rights and Freedoms were the Canadian Human Rights Commission and the commission's provincial counterparts. These bodies predated the Charter's implementation by as much as fifteen years in some provinces, and their history of rulings had much to do with the evolution of the Supreme Court's decisions in equality cases. They had established the principle of substantive remedies for those who suffered discrimination and were the pioneers in making the idea of "rights" part of Canadian political culture.

When John Crosbie, Campbell's predecessor at Justice, stood up in the House in 1986 and promised amendments to the Canadian Human Rights Act, he was doing nothing more than reflecting the majority opinion of mainstream Canada. The amendments did not only pertain to sexual orientation, but to a whole range of issues, such as rights for the disabled, the elderly, and aboriginal people. These changes to the Act had been unanimously recommended by a parliamentary committee with the standard majority of Tory MPs. That suggests that, party ideologues notwithstanding, ordinary Tory MPs were supportive when given the opportunity to examine the reasonableness of guaranteeing people's rights.

Not so the leadership or the family caucus. Crosbie, on the far right of the party himself, and the rural members of the family caucus did everything possible to stall the amendments, especially those pertaining to sexual orientation, but even those that were meant to assist the disabled and other groups. Their ability to stall these reforms reveals their power. In the Tory caucus, those pre-occupied with "family values" wield power far beyond their numbers and even farther beyond what public opinion would justify. So great is the influence of this group of fifteen to twenty MPs that they managed to delay passage of Human Rights amendments for seven years. In December 1992, when Campbell finally ended the Tory stonewalling on the issue, the amendments she presented did not reflect the enormous, positive changes in Canadian attitudes towards human rights. Instead, they reflected the family caucus's objections to human rights.

On February 8, 1993, national and B.C. human rights organizations called a news conference in Campbell's Vancouver Centre riding to demand the withdrawal of the amendments. Their statement left no doubt how those working for human rights felt about the proposals. Shelagh Day, as NAC vice-president and Justice Committee chair, denounced the amendments as an attempt to reverse the tide of progressive rulings and reforms. "Not since the Social Credit government in B.C. wiped out the B.C. Human Rights Commission and eviscerated the B.C. Human Rights Code have we seen such a damaging package of amendments to a human rights law in this country. Governments usually amend human rights laws to inch rights forward, not to cut them back. But that's what this package does."[42]

Stephen Hammond of Outspoken, a B.C. group representing gays and lesbians, attacked the amendment for denying his members the right to family status. Mary Williams, vice-president of the B.C. Coalition for Persons with Disabilities, was similarly critical. "For years we have been asking for the Act to require that persons with disabilities be accommodated unless accommodation creates undue hardship ... the Supreme Court has a read 'a duty to accommodate' into the legislation. Now the ... Minister proposes to amend the Act to put accommodation in but with a standard that is weaker than that already set out by the courts."[43] A federal government employees representative pointed to this as another instance where the government, having lost in the courts on a rights issue, was moving to take the law backwards. "Years ago the Human Rights Commission issued binding guidelines [for] equal pay for work of equal value. The federal government ... challenged them in the courts and lost. Now the government proposes to give itself the power to revoke equal pay guidelines."[44]

Sunera Thobani, the new president of NAC, was a member of the South Asian Women's Action Network at the time. She drew attention to amendments that would "effectively exempt immigration matters from ... the Canadian Human Rights Act ... no complaint about discrimination in immigration decisions can be made if it relates to a refusal outside Canada to grant a permit or visa ..." Virtually all applications for entry into Canada are made from outside the country; therefore, complaints of discrimination based on race, sexual orientation or disabilities would simply not be accepted. Again, this was a matter on which the federal government had argued in court that the Human Rights Commission had no jurisdiction, and had lost on appeal. As Thobani stated it, "This is an unacceptable position for a country which holds itself out internationally as a leader in the human rights field."[45]

Some amendments were positive. The Human Rights Commission was permitted to deal directly with retaliation against complainants, allowing it to pay costs to complainants and ensuring that its Human Rights Tribunal members hearing cases were "... experienced in and sensitive to, human rights." But the overall effect of the amendments, in terms of protection, was regressive. In addition to the areas identified in the joint news conference, the amendments exempted the military from adhering to the Act's disability provisions, gave the government, rather than the Commission, the power to set guidelines for tribunals, and moved the initial appeal procedure from the Commission to the courts.

Campbell's announcement of the amendments caught rights activists off-guard. There was no warning, let alone consultations. It was clear that Campbell had no intention of serious consensus building with the groups and agencies most interested in the Human Rights Act. The package of amendments was presented as a *fait accompli*. Of course, there had been consultations six years earlier, under Crosbie. But since that time much of the jurisprudence had changed, and virtually every sector wanted to comment. One look at the amendments was enough to alarm the rights community.

Campbell's office was deluged with demands for substantive consultations and for time so that the various groups concerned could carefully analyze the amendments in the context of recent court decisions and other developments. Campbell was not prepared for any such interference. Under tremendous pressure and threats of a major public battle, however, she agreed to a one-day meeting. There would be no resources available for groups to assess the legislation and no time: some of the people invited to take part had just a few days' notice to get to Ottawa for the "consultation."

Kathleen Ruff was one of those attending. "People at the meeting decided the whole process was hopeless. There was no time to prepare, no information to go on, no means provided to examine the proposals. Campbell attended in the morning. We went around the table and one by one, native women, the disabled, racial minorities — all criticized the proposals and the process."[46] But Campbell responded with hostility. "She chastised us, accusing us of being impolite and was generally derogatory of all of us. She was completely contemptuous of the comments of the groups represented," recalls Ruff.[47] As with the cancellation of the Court Challenges Program, consultation and compromise were not on the agenda.

Kim Campbell's Justice

Campbell's record in the Justice Department with respect to human rights reveals more about her political philosophy and approach to government than anything else in her record. As Justice Minister, she confronted policies and institutions that were fundamentally at odds with her political philosophy. While her defenders might argue that much of what took place in the court battles between rights groups and her officials was simply unknown to her, she was ultimately responsible for the way those battles were fought. Most important, the women at the historic 1991 symposium made it clear to Campbell that they objected to the way Justice was dealing with Charter challenges. She heard very strong representation on this issue along with a whole list of recommendations.

That nothing was done (and in fact the government's litigation became *more* aggressive) can be explained in part by the fact that it is bureaucrats who run government departments. Ministers come and go. Yet Campbell had a reputation for getting along extremely well with her officials, and they had great respect for her. Had she wished to make changes — certainly had she wished to save the Court Challenges Program — she could readily have done so. That she did not choose to do so would seem to reflect her élitist view of government and democracy. Her record in Justice was not the result of haphazard decisions or ministerial negligence. This was a minister who paid attention and applied her principles. As Ken Norman states, "I think there's real integrity to her. She's not just here or there according to the moment. She has some real substance. But it is a substance that we need to recognize has a dark side with respect to what I consider to be Canada's clearly defined path. We are a country perhaps more than any other country in the world that needs to understand difference and respect it — and not to homogenize it and or use pressures to silence that difference. We are a country that is too far down that road to reverse course."[48]

Canadians need to look at Campbell's record on human rights and compare it to what she says she stands for and the kind of politics she wants to promote. Her promise is the "politics of inclusion." Her record belies that promise in many ways. If we mean by "inclusive" that the political process should involve people more directly — and that is what she says it means — then Campbell has to be judged as having completely failed to accomplish this in the area of human rights. People who found themselves in groups discriminated against by the dominant culture were asking to be no longer excluded from benefits others took for granted because of their sexual orientation, physical disability, age or gender. They were crying out for inclusion.

Campbell quite simply turned a deaf ear. With all these groups, she made no move to address their desire to be included. They had to turn to the courts. Even there she fought tooth and nail to keep them out. But even in the narrower political sense, she rejected inclusiveness decisively and repeatedly by resisting the appeals by groups of citizens to be heard and more fundamentally by adhering more to the marginal and mean-spirited vision of the country held by the family caucus than by that held by the vast majority of the population. When it came to choosing between including disadvantaged groups or including the family caucus, Campbell's choice was too often and too obviously the family caucus.

There are those who would argue that Campbell did as well as anyone could have done within a Tory government; indeed, that she did better than anyone else could have. That may well be true.

But if it is, then the degree to which Campbell can deliver on her promise of "inclusiveness" is so circumscribed by the caucus and cabinet that her promise is scarcely worthy of the name. The people Campbell will "include" first when it comes to policies for the country are the same ones she includes now — the caucus and other right-wing Conservatives whom she must please and to whom she may owe allegiance as a result of the leadership race.

Campbell campaigns for the Vancouver school board, October 1980. *(George Diak/Vancouver Sun)*

Campbell at the keyboard, 1983. *(Bill Keay/Vancouver Sun)*

Chairing a Vancouver school board meeting, 1983.
(Joshua Berson/Vancouver Sun)

Campbell at a Socred leadership delegate selection meeting, 1986. The others are (left to right) John Reynolds, Bill Vander Zalm and Bob Wenman.
(Jon Murray/Vancouver Sun)

Addressing the Social Credit convention in Whistler, July 1986, when she ran against Bill Vander Zalm. *(Canapress Photo Service)*

Social Credit nomination meeting, Point Grey, September 1986.
(Jon Murray/Vancouver Sun)

Former MP Pat Carney nominates Campbell to run in her Vancouver Centre
riding, October 1988. *(Steve Bosch/Vancouver Sun)*

The candidates for the riding of Vancouver Centre in the 1988 federal
election: Campbell (PC); Tex Enemark (Lib.); Johanna den Hertog (NDP).
(Les Bazso/The Province)

Campbell at Conservative headquarters in Vancouver during the election
campaign, 21 November 1988. *(Bill Keay/Vancouver Sun)*

Campbell with Don Mazankowski, then deputy prime minister, during the 1988 federal election campaign. *(Mark Van Manen/Vancouver Sun)*

Campbell's headquarters for the federal election campaign in 1988. *(Bill Keay/Vancouver Sun)*

Mulroney and Campbell at a Conservative Party banquet, 6 December 1992.
(M. Parry/Vancouver Sun)

Campbell with Michael Levy, her replacement as Socred candidate in the
Point Grey riding, January 1989. *(Peter Battistoni/Vancouver Sun)*

Remembrance Day, 1991. *(Peter Battistoni/Vancouver Sun)*

The newly appointed Defence Minister inspects the Guard of Honour at CFB Esquimalt in January 1993. *(Peter Blashill/Vancouver Sun)*

Campbell announces her candidacy for the leadership of the Tory party in Vancouver, 25 March 1993. *(Ian Smith/Vancouver Sun)*

Campbell, Charest and Edwards smile for the cameras following a candidates' forum in Edmonton, April 1993. *(Ray Giguere/Canapress)*

Lissa Vroom congratulates her daughter at the announcement of her candidacy. *(Ian Smith/Vancouver Sun)*

Campbell with her father, George T. Campbell, at Vancouver International Airport, 24 March 1993. *(Nick Didlick/Vancouver Sun)*

A victorious Campbell acknowledges the crowd at the leadership convention, 13 June 1993. *(Canapress)*

Broken Promises

Many commentators on Kim Campbell's political career observed that despite her evident intelligence and political astuteness she seldom made her mark on the policies of the governing bodies in which she worked. This comment is particularly true of her tenure on the Vancouver school board, but it is also true of her time with the Social Credit party and government. Her opponents suggest that she has been so busy maintaining a high profile in her climb up the political ladder that she has had little time to pursue policies that she feels strongly about.

Before she joined the federal cabinet, Campbell did not have a great deal of authority or power to implement policies. Nevertheless, she held the Justice portfolio for three years — longer than most cabinet ministers are given to put their stamp on a department and certainly a sufficient tenure to do so. As we have seen, Campbell developed the reputation for getting along well with her bureaucrats in Justice and gaining their co-operation. These factors, together with her reputation for political toughness and savvy, should have given her a good opportunity to pursue the objectives close to her heart.

In interviews, Campbell has stated that she had clear objectives for herself in Justice. She told *The Globe and Mail*'s Graham Fraser in December 1992 that when she came to the department "I defined three priorities: protection of society, fairness in the relationship between citizens and government and inclusive justice."[1] The notion of "inclusive justice" comes up a lot in Campbell's description of what she wanted to accomplish — and believes she has accomplished — in her portfolio. She told Charlotte Gray, "The justice system must be inclusive: it must reflect the realities of all Canadians, as opposed to myths people have [about how women live] or outmoded assumptions."[2]

In earlier interviews she identified other objectives she had set for herself, "I want to leave a legacy in the job. There are issues on which I'd like to put my own stamp, such as juvenile justice...

In Justice we can have particular angles on this government's concern with the family. How do changes in the divorce law, for instance, affect the welfare of wives and children?"[3]

Another major goal for Campbell was the reform of "judicial attitudes towards women." She did not indicate just how she would accomplish this, yet that is not for lack of policy alternatives. She received very strong recommendations from the 1991 Vancouver symposium on women, the law and the justice system, including not only the appointment of more women judges, but also efforts to change the gender bias that is prevalent among sitting male judges, prosecutors and the police.

Campbell's own assessment of her accomplishments is quite generous. She cites gun control legislation as a major achievement, alongside amendments to the Criminal Code for mentally disordered offenders and changes to the Young Offenders Act and the Extradition Act. Oddly, she does not refer to how the public or outside observers may perceive her accomplishments. She looks instead to her own bureaucrats. "I'm told by my officials that I've produced an enormous amount of legislation since I've been here ... there's a major legacy there in terms of what's been done."[4]

The civil servants in Justice evidently admired Campbell. "After she delivered a legal analysis of the Charlottetown accord to a senior management meeting of her department, the civil servants — who have seen many a minister come and go — gave her a standing ovation."[5] But Campbell's pointed reference to their assessment of her performance as Justice Minister is not just unusual; it may reveal how distant she is from the public she is serving, particularly those groups that had an interest in what her department was doing about the issues affecting them. The judgement of these groups — including human rights activists, gays and lesbians, and equality-seeking groups — is not nearly so generous. And it is after all the judgement of the public that counts in a democracy, especially for someone who claims to champion inclusiveness.

While she does not refer explicitly to how the public viewed her actual accomplishments, Campbell repeatedly refers to her success at bringing new people into the process of making legislation. She told Graham Fraser that she believed that "inclusive justice" had become "an ethos and a value that has permeated the department."[6] She wants to use her Justice record to provide the

evidence of her commitment to inclusiveness. "On firearms legislation, on sexual assault legislation, and aboriginal justice, we've
learned that we can seek solutions together. Our challenge is not
just to define good policies, it's to bring people to the table."[7]

Campbell did, as her officials assured her, get an impressive
amount of legislation through Parliament in her three years as
minister. Quantity aside, how we judge this record is another
matter. In part, it is fair to judge it by comparing it to the objectives
she set out at the beginning of her tenure: juvenile justice, the
elimination of gender bias in the system, the protection of citizens
and inclusive justice.

We should also judge Campbell's record by how well it coin-
cides with what the majority of Canadians support in terms of
change: how does it correspond to the expressed needs and requests of the social groups affected by the law? Many would judge
that a harsh standard to meet, given that Campbell is part of a
Conservative Party government. She should, it is argued, be
judged on the basis of what she was able to get passed through a
very tough and intransigent caucus and a cabinet dominated by
right-wing men.

Perhaps. But Campbell is, after all, in the Conservative Party
and if, tough fighter that she is, she can only do as well as the
most right-wing of her colleagues will allow, that same rule is
likely to prevail if Canadians elect her prime minister. That she
was trying to get legislation through barriers presented by a vis-
cerally reactionary faction is not an aberration: it is the norm.
Campbell will need to have the support of her caucus and cabinet
in order to govern. A prime minister has debts to pay, regional
caucuses to placate and ideological balances to maintain.

Of the major areas of legislation that were dealt with during
Campbell's tenure as Justice Minister, abortion, sexual assault and
gun control probably received the most public attention. Yet none
of the legislation was initiated by Campbell. The existing abortion
legislation was struck down in 1988 by the Supreme Court after
a decade-long battle by pro-choice groups to change the law to
reflect not only public opinion but also the rights of women under
the Charter. The gun control issue was forced onto the agenda after
the misogynous slaughter of fourteen women students at the École
Polytechnique in Montreal on December 6, 1989. And the sexual
assault law was given priority when the Supreme Court decided

that the rules preventing reference to a woman's sexual history in a sexual assault trial were too restrictive.

These three issues more than any others allow an examination of Campbell's record as a Conservative and a feminist. On abortion, Campbell was already on record as supporting women's right to choose. During her Social Credit days, she had confronted her boss, Premier Bill Vander Zalm, on the issue publicly; there is no doubt that she really does believe that it is a woman's business whether or not she has a child. There is nothing to suggest that Campbell has ever been opposed to gun control. And there can be no doubt that she wants the legal system to give women effective protection against violence.

That Campbell held these positions personally provides us with a real test of what is possible under a Tory régime on these and other cultural and rights issues. They reveal just what the limits are under a Conservative government. Campbell — tough, bright, with the known confidence of Brian Mulroney and with public opinion firmly behind her on all three issues — was the best placed of any Tory to make significant progress.

Gun Control

The issue of gun control has never really gone away in Canada. Groups with an immediate interest — police forces in particular — have spent years lobbying government quietly for improvements in the law. But on December 6, 1989, the issue came back to the forefront with a terrible vengeance in the aftermath of the Montreal massacre. The horrific slaughter of fourteen women students galvanized public opinion against the easy acquisition of firearms, especially military assault rifles like the one used by Marc Lépine in Montreal. Within days of the murders, the students at the École Polytechnique started a petition calling for a ban on assault weapons. In less than four months they presented one of the largest petitions in Canadian history to Campbell, who was then Justice Minister: 560,000 people had signed on. Polls showed that 72 percent of Canadians supported tougher gun laws. Gun control became an issue the government could not ignore.[8]

People took up the gun control issue with the passion of those who have had a revelation. One of the key organizers of the movement was Wendy Cukier, a teacher at Ryerson Polytechnical Institute in Toronto. "I'm not particularly political but this situation was a real no-brainer. We have more control over dogs in big cities than we do over guns. Sixteen-year-olds could get guns without their parents knowing, and not just one gun — as many as they wanted. They couldn't buy cigarettes or a case of beer but they could buy an AK-47 and unlimited ammunition." [9] Within a month the government had introduced legislation, Bill C-80. But it lacked the very thing that police forces had been lobbying for and petitioners had demanded for over ten years: a ban on assault rifles. This essential feature would continue to elude the gun control movement for another year and a half.

Following the introduction of the bill, a group formed the previous January 1990, Canadians for Gun Control (CGC), issued a stinging report focusing on the bill's failure to ban assault weapons. By this time Campbell was Minister of Justice. She had problems of her own: Alberta MPs and rural MPs from other provinces were mounting fierce opposition to *any* gun control legislation. In order to pacify them and reason the bill through, she appointed the Canadian Advisory Council on Firearms. Ten of its fifteen members were gun owners. [10]

Three months later, in November 1990, Bill C-80, flawed as it was according to gun control advocates, failed to pass second reading because of the fierce opposition from Alberta and rural MPs. Gun control activists stepped up their campaign with a national letter-writing campaign and a joint letter from the families of Lépine's victims. They had been unprepared for the defeat of the bill. Cukier admitted that in the early stages the gun control movement was naïve, believing that the horror of the massacre would reinforce the simple logic of the demand for gun control. They were not ready for the massive letter-writing campaign of the other side, nor could they match the resources of the gun lobby, which allowed that group to hire over a dozen full-time lobbyists at the height of the struggle.

But while Canadians for Gun Control was slower off the mark than their opposition, they soon made up for it. They forced the parliamentary committee holding hearings into the new legislation, known as Bill C-17, to allow the families of Lépine's victims to testify. They even had an impact on some Tories. Before the release of the committee's report, Pierrette Venne, Conservative MP and the committee's vice-chair, publicly criticized the committee's work as defending the interests of gun owners as opposed to the public interest. Yet, in spite of Venne's efforts and the work of the gun control advocates, the committee produced recommendations that would further weaken the bill.[11]

In April 1991, Canadians for Gun Control joined with the students of the École Polytechnique to form the Coalition for Gun Control, a group that eventually came to include scores of organizations and civic agencies: city councils, police associations, boards of education, universities, the Canadian Association of Chiefs of Police, churches, hospitals and other health and health professionals' organizations, and many women's organizations, including women's shelters.[12]

By April 1991, the polls showed that the number of Canadians favouring stronger gun control legislation had risen to 80 percent. In May, the Coalition held a news conference at which it launched a multifaceted national campaign, including a mass postcard mailing to MPs and a nation-wide public-awareness drive.

Early on, the Coalition made a deliberate decision to spend a lot of time in Alberta. The Coalition knew that the most ferocious opposition to new legislation came from rural areas and from Alberta. They were determined to show that even here there was broad public support. In fact, they pointed out, 70 percent of Albertans supported tougher legislation. "We went across the country and deliberately went to rural ridings — to Vegreville, Alberta, and Williams Lake, B.C. Once they got over their initial antipathy towards people from central Canada, once we got down to basic elements — like do you think that anyone really needs an AK-47 — even gun owners supported a ban on military weapons," recalls Wendy Cukier.[13]

Cukier and Heidi Rathjen, a student at the École Polytechnique and the Coalition's executive director, were the two main organizers of the movement and eventually received an international award for their efforts. They emphasize that their objectives were carefully worked out and pragmatic. "We took as moderate a position as we could see would accomplish basic controls, the kind of controls you see over automobiles, and at the same time not inconvenience hunters and target shooters. We were not trying to eliminate guns in Canada. What we did was talk to the experts — the police, the criminologists — and eventually developed a position which was supported by the Canadian Association of Police Chiefs, the Public Health Association, the United Church and many others."[14]

The objectives of the Coalition reflected these moderate goals and constituted a critique of the existing law. They sought a complete ban on all military weapons in private hands, controls on the purchase of ammunition and the requirement that purchasers have a certificate for every gun acquired. The existing law required one permit, which entitled people to buy as many guns as they wanted. The law also allowed owners to keep weapons originally permitted only for target shooting even if the owner was no longer a *bona fide* target shooter. The Coalition sought rules enforcing safe storage of weapons, public education about the dangers of armed self-protection and a permit and checking system that would be self-financing.

The Coalition actually managed to win the support of a significant number of hunters and target shooters. But they discovered that the opposition they faced was more high-powered than they had expected. "If you look at the power base [of the opposition], who are the people who want military weapons, it's the target shooters, who are some of the richest, best connected people in the gun-owning community. There are at least two Queen's Counsel lawyers who represent the gun lobby. They have fourteen paid lobbyists working in Ottawa ... They get millions from their catalogue sales and they appeared in Ottawa at every hearing to speak against us," said Cukier.[15]

Campbell gave every sign of wanting to consult with the Coalition and Cukier is convinced that she supported stricter controls. While Campbell herself "wasn't particularly accessible," she apparently made it clear to her civil servants and political staff that the Coalition was to be consulted. As Cukier recalls, "They really did work at consulting with us and keeping us informed, at least going through the motions of consulting with us."[16]

But Campbell had enormous problems among her caucus members. In June 1991, just after Bill C-17 passed first and second reading, Campbell indicated that she wanted the parliamentary committee to pass the legislation without any amendments. She feared weakening amendments from her caucus members on the committee, but the Coalition was determined to fight for amendments to improve the bill. The parliamentary committee decided to go ahead with hearings and call witnesses.

The hearings began in September. A group of Tories led by Alberta MP Jim Hawkes was ruthless in its determination to prevent any changes to the current legislation. As Tory Whip,

Hawkes had a great deal of power, including a say over which Tories would sit on the committee. Just before the committee was to begin its hearings, Hawkes made last-minute substitutions of MPs considered to be gun control supporters. Four of the eight new members were from Alberta and six represented rural ridings. Hawkes was ultimately unable to gut the bill, but the legislation as finally presented after the committee hearings contained few of the improvements sought by the Coalition for Gun Control.

Asked what they got as a result of their two-year struggle for reform, Wendy Cukier immediately answered "Nothing!" Then she quickly backed off that position, despite her disappointment. "We did get stricter screening. The police can get references and even do community checks if they want. And the age restriction was raised from 16 to 18. The burden of proof that a permit should be given now rests on the applicant and not on the police as before, and that is significant."[17]

But what they did not get was most of what they fought hardest for. "We didn't get registration, we didn't get controls on ammunition sales, we didn't get cost recovery and we didn't get a ban on military weapons. The Ruger Mini-14 used to kill the women in Montreal is still legal and so is the AK-47." In addition, the Coalition request that permits be required for possession of weapons, as opposed to purchase alone, was rejected.

Cukier and others continued to express ambivalence about the legislation that finally passed the House of Commons. "What the Coalition wanted was reasonable, moderate, what would be supported by most people. What we got was some minor improvements. But the gun lobby fought them all, so the fact that we got anything at all was a defeat for the gun lobby."[18]

The Coalition's assessment of Campbell's role is equally ambivalent. They give Campbell credit for sticking it out when she could have backed off. "She did it despite the fact she had leadership ambitions or because she had leadership ambitions," says Cukier. "In terms of caucus it was an Alberta-Quebec split. I spoke to Al Johnson, a Calgary Tory MP, and he told me in the summer of '91, 'Campbell wants to be prime minister and this is as far as she can go.' "[19]

Heidi Rathjen agrees. "She's very sly in terms of packaging what she's doing to make it seem like it's answering everybody's concerns. What I remember clearly was that after the original bill [C-80] got struck down and she introduced the new one, she did not want any amendments — especially tougher ones. She said go ahead and toughen it up if you can but she won't go any further than the committee or the caucus will allow her to go, she won't push past that even if she has public support."[20]

Heidi Rathjen and Wendy Cukier, who maintained a scrupulous non-partisanship throughout the campaign, are in an especially good position to judge Campbell's claim to inclusive politics. "It makes me smile every time I hear her saying, 'Involve the people more,'" says Rathjen. "The whole point during the discussion around gun controls was that the public and the people who know about crime prevention and safety all wanted these basic changes. If you're talking about democracy and common sense then those two factors were completely ignored."[21] Says Cukier, "I would have to say she went as far as she could; on the other hand, she is a Conservative. In all that stuff she says about feminism, and about accommodation, she is constrained by her party."[22]

Abortion

Campbell's initial public reputation as a feminist and her principal claim to that status rested almost exclusively on her pro-choice position on abortion. She very publicly confronted her former boss, Bill Vander Zalm, on the issue. She did not hesitate to identify herself with a woman's right to an abortion and the state's obligation to pay for it. Consequently, when she was appointed Justice Minister in February 1990 and faced a bill that would recriminalize abortion, she was presented with a real test.

In 1988, the Supreme Court had declared the old abortion bill to be in violation of the Charter of Rights and Freedoms on the grounds that it threatened women's right to security of the person both psychologically and physically by forcing them to go through a process that necessitated significant delays. The constraint on women's ability to act on their own, in their own interests, was found to have a harmful impact on their health. Yet in spite of this ruling and her own stated position on abortion, in November 1989 Campbell passionately defended the new legislation to recriminalize abortion, well before any rumour of a cabinet shuffle and well outside her responsibilities in Indian Affairs. We cannot know whether she defended the bill as a way of signalling that she was interested in the position of Justice Minister or whether she was simply demonstrating her loyalty. What we do know is that she defended the recriminalization of abortion with great zeal. On issue after issue, she defended it with a determination that startled every group involved, from criminal lawyers to constitutional experts, the medical profession, editorialists and both sides of the abortion debate.

Campbell had been barely sworn in as Justice Minister before she began putting forth the line she would use unswervingly for many months to come. Her arguments in favour of recriminalization prompted *The Toronto Star* to editorialize: "Less than a week in office and Justice Minister Campbell is drumming up specious arguments to justify a government bill to put abortion back into the criminal code."[23] The "specious argument" *The Star* was referring to was the assertion that if the government did not put abortion back in the Criminal Code the provinces would be free to severely restrict access to abortion.[24] It was classic Campbell, according to Shelagh Day. "This debate showed something that Campbell was really good at, and that is turning arguments around backwards in order to make herself look liberal when in fact she is promoting something very regressive. She did exactly the same thing when she put sexual orientation in the human rights act."[25]

Campbell's second argument was equally dubious. She stated that requiring medical justification for legal abortions would create a "national standard of entitlement" to abortion for Canadian women.[26] It was another example of turning an argument around backwards. But neither this position nor the argument about preventing provincial actions held water. And the women's movement, well endowed with legal expertise, knew it.

The National Association of Women and the Law (NAWL) wrote repeatedly to Campbell over a period of months asking for her department's legal analysis supporting these interpretations. None was forthcoming. To try to force her hand, NAWL wrote letters to constitutional experts across the country, asking them for their analysis of Campbell's arguments. They were answered with a flood of responses supporting their contention that the minister's arguments were legal flimflam. Of eighteen replies, only one supported Campbell. The rest ranged from critical to contemptuous of Campbell's position. Constitutional legal scholars from Osgoode Hall, McGill, the University of Western Ontario, UBC, the University of Ottawa and the University of Victoria all declared Campbell's interpretation to be wrong. Bruce Ryder of Osgoode Hall said, "These arguments are legal nonsense. Firstly,

Bill C-43 does not create a national standard of legal entitlement to abortion ... Secondly, [it] will do nothing to remove the provinces' ability to place restrictions on funding and access to abortion." Law professors Hester Lesard and Andrew Petter of Victoria described the arguments as "untenable ... a federal law does not render a provincial law occupying the same field untenable. An exemption from criminal law ... is not an entitlement." Others used terms such as "disingenuous," "unconvincing in law and in fact," "constitutionally ill-founded." Professor Donna Greschner of the University of Saskatchewan wrote, "This [jurisdictional] argument is also fallacious and does not represent a sound interpretation of constitutional law principles." Professors Martha Jackman and Sandra Rogers from the University of Ottawa pointed out that "a provincial law which could be characterized as criminal in nature would be unconstitutional, regardless of federal criminal abortion law."[27]

Campbell maintained her position. Despite having received the legal opinions of the eighteen constitutional legal scholars, she stood in the House and declared that she had seen only the newspaper reports of the opinions; in any case, she said, she was sticking to her views, pointing out that one of the opinions agreed with hers.[28] She continued to use the same arguments, holding in effect that for women to be assured of access to abortion, it would have to recriminalized. Campbell's department never did provide a legal analysis of her position.

The legal arguments back and forth had little impact on the general public, given their esoteric nature and the polarized character of the debate. But if disputes between Campbell and legal experts had little impact on the public perception of the bill, the mounting fear on the part of physicians who performed abortions was well publicized. The bill provided for jail sentences of up to two years for doctors performing abortions when the mental, physical or psychological health of the mother was not endangered. Women receiving illegal abortions could also be jailed.

Newspapers across the country began running stories about the many doctors who were already refusing to do abortions simply on the threat of the legislation passing. In August 1990, the Canadian Abortion Rights Action League (CARAL) wrote to Campbell with a list of doctors from Brantford, Brockville, Scarborough, Sault Ste Marie, Winnipeg, Calgary, Edmonton and Victoria who had either stopped providing abortions or who had announced that they would do so on the day the legislation passed.[29] In September, *The Toronto Star* reported the results of a survey of obstetricians and gynaecologists which showed that 200 of the 700 doctors then performing abortions in Canada had already stopped performing abortions or would stop if the bill became law. The head of the Society of Obstetricians and Gynaecologists declared that, in the event of the bill's passage, "women would have even more problems getting access to abortion." [30]

Campbell's response was identical to her reply to the eighteen constitutional experts: she stonewalled. She maintained that her interpretation was correct: the doctors had nothing to fear because provincial attorneys-general would not tolerate "frivolous" prosecutions. But she as much as admitted that doctors' concerns were legitimate by advising them to band together and refuse to be intimidated, and to sue troublemakers for malicious prosecution.[31]

While Campbell was telling doctors not to worry about pro-lifers, groups opposed to abortion were publicly declaring that they would be using the courts to intimidate doctors. Alliance for Life, the umbrella anti-abortion group, stated that if the law were passed "our route would be to go to the doctors." They would also consider financing individuals trying to block abortions by suing doctors privately.[32] The doctors' concerns were backed by their own associations, including the Canadian Medical Association, as well as by the Criminal Lawyers Association (CLA). Paul Copeland of the CLA stated, "The minister's demonstrated lack of knowledge of the Criminal Code leaves me regarding her reassurances as virtually worthless." [33] The doctors' own associations advised that they might have to get second opinions when they recommended abortions and/or insist on "psychological evaluation and ... psychiatric consultation" [34] for patients. Both courses of action would delay women's access to abortion, the very problem the Supreme Court identified as cause for striking down the old abortion law. Still Campbell would not budge. Facing growing opposition to the bill in the Senate, she mounted an impassioned defence of the bill before the Senate committee studying the legislation. Standing the concept of democracy on its head, Campbell told the senators, "If we allow those who would thwart the will of parliament, who would abuse the system, to prevent us from exercising our power ... then I think we have seen an enormous defeat for democracy and parliamentary government." [35]

This statement flew in the face of virtually unanimous opposition to the bill from every conceivable organization with any interest in it. Of fifty-two organizations that presented evidence before the Commons committee, forty-six had opposed the bill outright and two others were uncertain of their position. Yet no amendments were allowed.[36] In addition, Campbell readily admitted her certainty that the bill's constitutionality would be called into question. "I am quite convinced that it will be subject to challenge. I think there is no question of that," she told the Senate committee.[37]

Campbell's statement that democracy would suffer a blow if the bill were defeated was absolutely consistent with her right-wing, majoritarian view of Parliament. The government, once elected, had the authority and the power to implement legislation regardless of public opinion or the views of any other group. There is little doubt that Campbell really believed that any challenge to that kind of power and authority was a violation of democracy. Yet her defence of Bill C-43 seemed to go beyond even this Burkean standard. Her combativeness was far more than just a minister's duty to see a piece of legislation through to the end. Even the most rigid adherent of the Westminster model of parliamentary democracy admits the legitimacy of the amendment process. Here Campbell was demonstrating her toughness under fire and her ability to turn an argument on its head, and she was demonstrating these qualities for Brian Mulroney.

Bill C-43 went down to defeat in a free vote in the Senate. If there was any doubt that Campbell really wanted the legislation to pass the Senate, it was removed when she phoned her friend Pat Carney and berated her for voting against the bill. Carney, who had preceded Campbell as Conservative MP in Vancouver Centre, had flown to Ottawa, in spite of illness, to vote against it. The bill failed to pass on a tie vote, and Campbell chose to blame Carney for the defeat.

The Rape Shield Law

Examining what Campbell accomplished on abortion, the gun control issue and the rape shield law is an instructive comparison for those wishing to assess this particular Conservative. For these were three issues that seemed to separate Campbell from most other Tories. In looking at these issues, we can see clearly the extent to which Campbell was willing to subordinate her political philosophy and principles when it came to pleasing her caucus or advancing her career.

This is not as obvious a point as it might seem. Certainly all political leaders must, in a parliamentary system, accommodate different views in their caucus if they are to accomplish anything. But what is significant here is that it was a Tory caucus that Campbell had to accommodate as a minister and it will be a Tory caucus she will constantly have to accommodate as prime minister. For those looking for a different kind of Tory, a kinder, gentler Tory, this fact is of the utmost importance. Combine it with an assessment of how much Campbell departs, if at all, from the traditional practices of a political party — including patronage and paying off political debts — and we have a good reading of what we can ultimately expect from Prime Minister Campbell.

Of all the issues that Campbell dealt with in her Justice portfolio, the rape shield law was the one clear case where women's groups and feminists in general gave her high marks. There was genuine consultation with the women's movement on effective protection for victims of sexual assault, sincere effort on Campbell's part to actually respond to the Supreme Court's decision to throw out the rape shield provisions, and a willingness to change her mind and act on that change.

Judy Rebick, the outspoken former head of the National Action Committee on the Status of Women (NAC) and general nemesis of everything Tory, recalls the developments around the rape shield issue vividly. "When the law was struck down, women's groups got together to see what we could do about it. Since the court had ruled that the 'shield' in the old law [which prevented defence council from referring to a victim's sexual history] was unconstitutional, we had to come up with a strategy for finding another way in the law to protect women. We concluded that the way to do that was to define consent in such a way that a woman's past sexual history would almost never be relevant."[38]

It seemed an effective way to answer the court's concern that defendants were being denied access to all possible avenues of defence. But most of the women's groups thought their chances of getting such a provision in the new law to be very slight. They knew that Campbell was moving to replace the old law and they soon discovered that she was in a hurry to do so. She wanted to pass the legislation in the current sitting of Parliament.

The original strategy of the women's organizations was to do everything they could to delay the legislation, anticipating a long and difficult fight to get the provision they wanted. That provision — which came to be known as the "no means no" provision — removed from the defence arsenal against an accusation of rape the common plea that the man believed that the woman was consenting to the sexual act. It was a radical departure from the current thinking and would break new ground in confronting gender bias in the law. Given their experience with the Tory government and with Campbell, the women's organizations were not optimistic.

In the fall of 1992, they met first with Justice officials, who rejected the suggested provision as virtually impossible as a response to the Court's decision. It might be adopted some time in the future, but there was no hope of considering it this time around. At that point, the women's groups insisted on a meeting with Campbell.

Campbell, according to Rebick, came into the meeting believing that there were fundamental differences between her and the feminists she would be confronting. Her goal was to get legislation onto the books as quickly as possible; theirs was to delay the writing of the legislation so that they could eventually help draft it. "But," says Rebick, "what happened was that in the course of the meeting she listened to us, changed her mind and took action right there. She completely switched gears."[39]

Campbell opened the meeting by stating her position: the approach of her department would be to codify the decision of the Supreme Court and to set up strict guidelines for judges dealing with sexual assault cases. She insisted that a new law had to be passed in the current session. The women's representatives responded with their ultimatum. If Campbell went ahead with the planned legislation as described she would face fierce opposition from every women's group in the country as well as the Canadian Bar Association.

"We outlined what we wanted to see in the new legislation. It was not fully developed but it was clear in its intent and the legal basis for it was there. To our astonishment she said, 'We're not that far apart, I think we can work this out.' She still was not willing to delay introduction of the new legislation."[40] The meeting moved quickly on to the process that would be followed in getting the women's groups' provisions into the legislation. The women's groups insisted that they continue to meet with the department's bureaucrats on the issues, but also made it clear that they had to consult with about sixty women's organizations who had a direct interest in the law, to ensure a legitimate process. Campbell agreed to the process.

As the meeting ended, Campbell made it clear to her officials that this was how it was going to be. They were to take the advice of the women and the organizations they represented in drafting the amendments to their own legislation.

The officials, said Rebick, were not at all happy. "They were basically told that they had to listen to us. We were not just consulting, we were going to be involved in actually drafting the new bill. And we were doing it with a process that we had insisted on."[41]

Rebick, Sheila MacIntyre and Joanne St. Lewis of the Women's Legal Education and Action Fund (LEAF), Ann Derrick, a criminal lawyer from Halifax and the other women at the meeting were concerned that their victory might fade away once the bureaucrats got hold of the process — and the minister. To solidify their remarkable achievement, they decided to call a news conference that same day to announce the result of the meeting. It turned out to be a brilliant tactic.

Rebick was the first to speak. "I stated that we went in expecting to be far apart on our positions but that instead we had reached agreement with the minister. No one in the media had ever heard me praise the Tories before, so that got their attention right away. Then Sheila [MacIntyre] outlined what we had presented as our proposals for the bill. She did not say that this was what we had agreed upon but that impression was left with all but a few reporters. I explained the 'no means no' concept in the law."[42]

The effect of the story was to give Campbell probably the best press she had ever had as Justice Minister. She was given front-page coverage in many papers, including *The Globe and Mail*. "I honestly do not know if she would have actually gone ahead with it if we had not established it in the media as an accomplished fact. But in any case, she got such good publicity from it that she could not turn it down."[43]

In the end, the "no means no" provision was included in the new legislation, as Campbell had promised. The women's organizations did not get everything they wanted. They had sought additional clauses recognizing that women in certain groups —

women of colour, prostitutes and the disabled — faced additional barriers when it came to sexual assault trials, but here Campbell would not budge. "As far as she was concerned this just was not an issue. Her response was that all women experience violence, period. She just would not accept it — she did not even seem to understand it. It reflected her élitist view of women's problems and her own class background," said Rebick.[44]

The other defeat, in the eyes of some women, was the actual definition of consent. LEAF and others had pressed very hard for a definition of unequivocal consent as the basis for "no means no." They did not get it.

Rebick gives full credit to Campbell for the new rape shield legislation, but points out something that Campbell herself admitted before the negotiations even got underway. And that was that Campbell did not have to fight to get the bill passed. "There was no obstacle in her path. She told us from the beginning that she had support from the cabinet and the caucus."[45]

Ironically, the law has turned out to be much less effective than its drafters had initially hoped. Defence lawyers are now using pre-trial hearings to bring up references to the victim's sexual history, effectively circumventing the law. That is why women active in equal rights issues have turned their attention to attacking the gender bias in the administration of justice. Says Rebick, "What's the use of changing the laws if the people in charge of applying them are biased against those the law is supposed to help?"[46]

Ridding the System of Gender Bias

In numerous interviews Campbell stated that one of her principal goals as Justice Minister was to deal with the pressing issue of bias in the judicial system. She told Charlotte Gray that it was her plan to reform judicial attitudes towards women.[47] And at the Vancouver symposium, Women, Law and the Administration of Justice, she put the issue at the top of her priorities.

Campbell, the first Justice Minister to acknowledge publicly that the system was sexist, was pledging to do something about it. Her pledge was made to some of the most able and influential feminist activists in the country. And they took her at her word. The Vancouver symposium was probably unprecedented in that it brought together a Justice Minister asking for input and the feminist legal community who were prepared to do the work to accomplish just that. In the words of Shelagh Day: "It was absolutely clear what our thoughts were about reforming the system to get rid of gender bias. There were no excuses. The ball was in her court." [48]

The women at the Vancouver meeting judged it a success not because of promises made by Campbell, but because it had been a unique opportunity for women to sit down and work out detailed recommendations on how to make the judicial system fairer. "The meeting was actually very badly organized, but we asked for and got extra time to meet," said Day. "We formed a sort of ad hoc coalition on the spot and got together, did a lot of work and produced some really comprehensive and coherent recommendations. The most important outcome from the symposium in my view was that women felt that they had the opportunity to be on the record with the minister to say what the scope of the problems were for women in the justice system. We felt we had made our mark: she could not possibly be confused or misunderstand what the problems were. From then on we would wait to see what she was prepared to do."[49]

Campbell had promised even before the symposium to address the problem of gender bias in the system. At the symposium the issue was addressed from every possible perspective, "not just with the existing judges on the bench but with appointments, procedures, with interpretation, with what the federal government itself was saying in court on issues of equality, how crown prosecutors were behaving — the whole gamut of how gender bias works its way through the system," explained Day.[50]

The recommendations that emerged, reinforced by further representations by NAC, LEAF and other women's organizations, gave the government clear direction, according to Judy Rebick. "The key recommendations put forward suggestions for affirmative action on the bench, a more transparent disciplinary system for judges — the judicial councils are secretive, inaccessible boys' clubs made up completely of other judges — mandatory judicial education as well as education at the police and prosecutors level, better co-ordination between criminal justice and social services, particularly with respect to battered women." [51]

Women's organizations hear from the frontline workers that reform of gender bias in the system is essential. Progressive legislation is necessary, but as long as the judicial system itself does not take the social issues behind the crimes seriously, it is not enough. Women's groups now point to 1993 proposals for an anti-stalking law (brought in after Campbell left Justice) as an example of how new laws simply are not an adequate way of addressing the problems faced by women in the system. "While it isn't yet clear," says Rebick, "it appears to make the test just how terrorized a woman is. So once again it will be the women who [are] on trial — trying to prove that they are terrorized enough to warrant action by the courts. The problem is not the law — it's that judges and police do not believe women." [52]

If there was one goal Campbell set for herself in which she could have made a tremendous difference, it was the elimination of gender bias in the system. But the record shows that it is here that the least has been done. According to Charlotte Gray in an article on Campbell in late 1991, the number of women in the judiciary actually declined during Campbell's first year and a half in the Justice portfolio.[53] While the last year and a half of her tenure at Justice saw many more appointments of women, it is still unclear whether most of these women are themselves committed to ending gender bias in the system. Some of the high-profile appointments have put prominent feminist legal activists such as Rosalie Abella on the bench, but the use of the judiciary for patronage is still prevalent.

According to constitutional expert Peter Russell, who describes himself as "obsessed" with the issue of patronage in the judiciary, the problem is far from solved. In a study of the first Mulroney administration, Russell found considerable political patronage among the 250 appointments. He is just completing a study of Mulroney's second government, beginning in 1988. "The bottom line would be that under [Campbell] the judicial appointments were marginally better than in the first administration in the sense that there were fewer of the really blatant political appointments. Of course I'm someone who thinks one is too many. It was clear that when the prime minister insisted on an appointment she was not willing to take him on." [54]

On the broader issue of reforming the way in which judges are appointed, Campbell's record is just as bad as those of her predecessors. "The Canadian Bar Association and the Canadian Association of Law Teachers have both lobbied vigorously for reforms in the way judges are appointed. [Campbell] was unwilling to accept their basic reform, which was to turn their advisory committees that they have in every province into real nominating committees. As they are now, these are just a basic camouflage for patronage." [55] Russell cites Ontario as the province that has set the standard for judicial appointments. Positions are advertised in legal journals and even in regular newspapers. A committee that includes lay people interviews candidates and recommends two or three of the very best for the province's attorney general to choose from. In fact, Ontario has gone even further. It is the first government in the country to make radical changes to the criteria and qualifications for judicial appointees. According to Judy Rebick, "they are appointing a majority of women and minorities, and one criterion is that people have some social justice experience. That is absolutely critical: you have to change the criteria for appointing judges if you want to get rid of gender, racial and class bias in the system. The old boys in Ontario are furious because they no longer qualify to be judges." [56]

Evidently, Campbell was not prepared to see the whole country's "old boys" furious over real changes to the judiciary. Despite her statement about sexism in the system, despite her stated goal of addressing it, little, save more female appointments, happened under her three-year tenure to reform the system. According to Day, "Very, very little has been done. It seems virtually unchanged as far as the women who actually experience the system on a day-to-day basis are concerned. We certainly cannot say that since the Vancouver symposium took place things have changed as a result." [57]

Campbell demonstrated in dramatic fashion that when she was moved to change things, she could do so decisively and without fear of using her authority with her own bureaucracy. Her willingness to change her mind on the "no means no" provision in the new rape shield law indicates that Campbell knew how to use power if she chose to. She simply ordered her officials to take their direction from the feminist community on the issue. But when it came to challenging the justice establishment, the "old boys' club" that has so much power in defining what justice really means in Canada, and when it came to eliminating the traditional system of handing out political favours, Campbell did nothing.

The Legacy

Campbell's own assessment of her record does not square with the assessment of others, not in terms of what she said she set out to do, not in reflecting the changes taking place in society that demanded action, nor even by the general standard that the changes she did implement were made on her own initiative. As NDP Justice critic Ian Waddell put it, "The fact is that most of the legislation has been reacting to the courts, and the government has been leaving it up to the courts and ducking these tough issues." [58]

Most of the major pieces of legislation implemented under Campbell's tenure as minister were forced on the government and Campbell by decisions of the courts. It was not at Campbell's initiative that new gun control laws were introduced, abortion removed from the criminal code, or the rape shield provision strengthened to protect women who had been sexually assaulted. In all these areas, Campbell appeared content with the status quo just as she appeared content with it on sexual orientation and human rights legislation, and on access for the disabled. Her legacy would have been thin indeed had it not been for the courts obliging her and her department to change the laws that the courts found lacking. Campbell takes credit for changes she did not initiate while simultaneously criticizing the courts for forcing her to make them.

Judged by her own statements about her goals as Justice Minister, Campbell's record is decidedly mixed. On working to eliminate the bias in the judicial system there was no initiative outside a few women appointed to the bench. On "inclusive justice" there was virtually no initiative that was hers alone. On the issue of gun control, it was a public outcry that led to her actions. On abortion, Campbell made every effort to recriminalize the procedure and take the country backwards. On the rape shield law, the progressive legislation was the result of the forceful demands of women's groups that she meet with them or face the consequences. In the area of aboriginal justice she steadfastly refused to consider a separate justice system, imposing her own élitist views in place of the virtually unanimous view of native people and the conclusion of several provincial government reports and public inquiries. Aboriginal people may have been at the table, but Campbell was not listening. As for land claims, she was prepared to dump her previous steadfast opposition to any notion of aboriginal entitlement because it is simply too archaic a view to express years after several federal governments had recognized aboriginal rights.

One of Campbell's other goals was to ensure "fairness in the relationship between the citizen and the state." [59] Again, in the area of discrimination, Campbell proved hostile to the notion of rights. Her amendments to the Human Rights Act represented a step backwards, away from fairness.

Other legislation that Campbell takes credit for includes a new juries act, which eliminated the prosecution's advantage in the selection of jury members, and the elimination of the use of lieutenant-governors' warrants to incarcerate mentally disturbed offenders indefinitely. In both cases, it was the courts that insisted on changes to the law because citizens were being treated unfairly by the state. Campbell knew of this unfairness, yet made no move to address it.

Another of Campbell's stated objectives as minister was "protecting society." [60] Yet in gun control, Campbell bowed to a small group of extreme reactionaries in her caucus and a lobby group for a wealthy and influential minority. Campbell was determined to protect her political base. But the gun that was used to massacre fourteen innocent women is still available for the next mass killer to use.

The single area in which Campbell pledged to act and has taken the initiative was in the broad area of protecting society. The new Young Offenders Act provides for harsher penalties. There is no doubt that there are young offenders who deliberately manipulate the more lenient laws that apply to them. But punitive changes to the way society deals with young offenders is one of the conservative right's favourite issues — and a major Reform Party initiative. That Campbell would pick this particular area of the law for her only completely independent initiative is consistent with her philosophical views that place "the rule of law" above all other principles of good government. As in many other areas of legislation, the Tories' motivation for changes to the Young Offenders Act may have been to try to regain supporters on the far right lost to Preston Manning's promise to get tough with youthful offenders.

Abusing Authority

Campbell has demonstrated that she is an accomplished politician of the old school: willing and able to manoeuvre the difficult waters of pleasing the factions in her party while appearing to respond to public demands. Ambitious for power, she has demonstrated her adeptness at using it and seeking it. Even when it comes to principles derived from "seeing the world differently as a woman," Campbell knows when she has to sacrifice principle for practicality and advantage. She has done so not only in legislation on abortion and gun control, but also in instances where she was faced with the dilemma of acting either in the interest of justice or in the interest of protecting her government from criticism.

One example of Campbell protecting the government is the Justice Department's apparent efforts to deny certain documents to the Westray Mine Public Inquiry. The inquiry was formed to look into all aspects of the tragedy that took the lives of twenty-six miners. Details discovered by the media indicated that the mining project had gone ahead despite strong advice against it from federal civil servants who believed the coal deposit in question was too dangerous to mine. Political interference from the highest levels of the Nova Scotia and federal governments had overridden the best technical assessment of the project.

On April 1, 1993, Cape Breton Liberal MP David Dingwall rose in the House to accuse Campbell of a cover-up. Campbell had refused to provide the Westray Inquiry with key documents. "I ask the ... Prime Minister if he would indicate to the house whether or not the then Minister of Justice was acting alone [in her refusal to provide documents] or acting in full concert and knowledge of the entire cabinet." [61]

Two days earlier, John Merrick, the counsel for the Westray Inquiry, had taken the dramatic step of issuing a news release revealing the federal government's refusal to release important documents to the inquiry. "The federal government has not released all of its Westray documents to the Inquiry. Specifically, the Inquiry does not have a copy of the memo to Energy, Mines and Resources Minister, Jake Epp, entitled Federal Funding of the Westray Coal Mine." This document was the key advisory memo to the government regarding whether or not funding should be provided.

Another document obtained from other sources was "incomplete" said the release — implying that it had been censored by the government. "Regrettably," said the news release, "the Inquiry had recently concluded that it had no option but to consider formal proceedings to resolve this matter." [62] In other words, the inquiry was considering taking Ottawa to court.

The missing document was the eighteen-page memo to Jake Epp from his deputy minister. The Liberals obtained the document through Freedom of Information, an act administered by the Justice Department, but received eighteen blank pages. The document had been censored through the use of the most powerful tool at the government's disposal — by order of the Privy Council or cabinet. Under this particular order, no judge of any court could get access to the document under any circumstances.

Even the date was blanked out. According to the Liberals, an anonymous source within the government dated the document in January 1990 — exactly at the time the government was facing the crunch in terms of a Yes or No to the funding request. The censorship of the document strongly suggested that the suspicions regarding a negative assessment were correct; otherwise it would not have been dealt with so decisively by cabinet.

The other document was called the Canmet report. It was a review of all the private feasibility studies done on the coal deposit at the Westray site. When it was released to the government in June 1992, it consisted of nine pages. But when it was released to the Liberals under Freedom of Information, the department noted that six additional pages of the report had been censored. It was this report that the Liberals focused on in their challenge in the House. The government simply denied that there were any other pages.

Campbell's role in the affair was established in a letter from the Head of the Inquiry, Mr. Justice K. Peter Richard, to Liberal David Dingwall. Responding to Dingwall's request for a listing of the relevant documents, Justice Richard implied that he had not received all the relevant documents despite promises to the contrary: "The order was served on the Government of Canada with notice to the Minister of Justice (through an Associate Deputy Minister) ... I was assured by the Associate Deputy Minister that the Federal Government would co-operate with the Inquiry." [63] The diplomacy in the letter aside, the implication was clear — the Justice Department had *not* co-operated.

In her role of protector, Campbell and her senior bureaucrats had many important Tories to protect in the Westray scandal. The key people helping get the project on track were: Peter White, Brian Mulroney's Principal Secretary at the time who made several interventions on behalf of the developers; Elmer MacKay, Campbell's fellow cabinet minister in whose federal riding the mine was located; Nova Scotia Premier Don Cameron; Mulroney's chief of staff, Stanley Hartt; and Robert Coates, the former defence minister forced to resign and a key Mulroney activist in the campaign to bring down Joe Clark.

Campbell's oft-repeated claim to have been the architect of a "major legacy" in Justice is simply not supported by the evidence. And that is as consistent as it is surprising. Her three years in Justice parallel in many ways her years on the Vancouver school board. In both instances Campbell, obviously bright and a quick learner, proved unable to create her own legacy, to put her own stamp on the institution she worked in. Phil Rankin, one of keenest observers of the Campbell phenomenon, may have come the closest to figuring out what makes Campbell tick and why she does not live up to her potential. According to Rankin, Campbell's priority never really has been accomplishing goals. It has been pleasing people.

"She desperately wants to be accepted by the establishment. She's not to the manner born, but she would like to be ... She's always performing because underneath it all she's a very lonely person. I think she's playing a character. But the trouble with playing a character is that it becomes a caricature and I think that's she very close to becoming a caricature now." [64]

Her record in Justice also speaks to another claim that Campbell makes again and again, and that is her repeated commitment to do politics differently as Canada's new prime minister. Yet throughout her tenure as Justice Minister her greatest accomplishment was playing the old, traditional politics so well: her ability to stand an issue on its head, her willingness to jettison her most important political principles to gain caucus support.

The Defence Portfolio

Mulroney's decision to make Kim Campbell Minister of Defence in January 1993 involved some high risks for her future candidacy as Tory leader. It also held out some potential benefits for Campbell. Defence was a portfolio that could help toughen up Campbell's image for those Tories who viewed her performance in Justice as too liberal. Photo opportunities of Campbell reviewing the troops might help counter the memory of her involvement with gun control legislation. The Canadian military's role in peacekeeping had been generally popular and was one of the features highlighted in government ads aired during the 1992 constitutional debate.

As Defence Minister, Campbell would have control over the budget that represents the largest amount of discretionary spending (what is left after fixed expenses, including transfers to the provinces) in the hands of federal politicians. Defence also has the largest capital spending budget of any federal department. In contrast with the cutbacks to other programs, Finance Minister Don Mazankowski's April 1993 budget protected the military from cuts for the foreseeable future. Since government support for military industries is one of the few areas of public subsidy permitted under the terms of the Canada–U.S. Free Trade Agreement, it is one of the few areas left where the federal government can prop up faltering regional economies.

All these factors mean potential advantages for Canadian Defence Ministers in the 1990s. While other ministers have to explain painful cuts or elimination of programs, the Defence Minister can announce new contracts to any number of communities that have become dependent on military spending. The recent practice of giving out billion-dollar contracts without tender allows considerable leeway for decisions to be made on the basis of where military spending will reap the greatest political reward.

The Controversial Legacy of Marcel Masse

Campbell was soon vulnerable to some of the political risks associated with the Defence portfolio. Marcel Masse, Campbell's predecessor in the Department of National Defence, took such blatant advantage of the department's spending potential to channel benefits to Quebec that he made defence procurement a highly controversial issue. In 1992, he ignored a consultant's report and relocated an Ontario military depot to Montreal. The consultant, who had recommended that the facility should go to Kingston, rated the Montreal site as the least desirable of the four possible options.[1]

Masse created a furor in April 1992 by giving a $1 billion untendered contract to Bell Textron of Mirabel, Quebec, for one hundred light-duty helicopters, double the number the Defence Department had originally requested. To the surprise of many military observers, Masse succeeded in July 1992 in pushing through early cabinet approval of yet another helicopter contract — this time for the EH101, the most expensive helicopter in the world. The EH101 purchase enabled Masse to bail out Paramax, the Montreal-based electronics firm that stood to benefit most from the deal. In one year, Masse had committed $7 billion to military helicopters. NDP MP Howard McCurdy quipped that the government had "a helicopter fetish."[2]

Masse's extravagance and Quebec bias as Defence Minister prompted even traditional defenders of the military to raise the alarm. Nicholas Stethem of the Strategic Analysis Group complained that Masse had "a lack of interest in defence, but an all-consuming interest in doing what he can for Quebec."[3] Richard Rohmer, *Toronto Sun* columnist and former major general, fulminated against Masse, calling him "that farce of a minister of national defence" and "a Quebec nationalist mouthpiece" who was discrediting the armed forces by these purchases.[4] A June 11, 1992, *Globe and Mail* editorial described Masse's approach to military spending as "pork by pop" and Canada's military procurement program as "out of control."

Masse demonstrated little concern for the political storm his actions were generating. As an avowed Quebec nationalist, he had declared that his first objective in being involved in politics at the federal level was getting the greatest benefit for Quebec.[5] In response to criticism that too many untendered defence contracts were going to his home province, Masse shot back during an April 1992 meeting of a parliamentary defence committee that he thought even more of Canada's defence dollar should be spent in Quebec. To those who questioned what the underlying security rationale was for these new contracts, Masse responded that his critics were guilty of the same "appeasement" policies that had allowed Hitler to rise to power. This accusation was greeted with derision by columnists who asked what Hitler-like enemy of Canada there was to appease in the post-Cold War era and confirmed that the Defence Minister had little understanding of the strategic issues of the day.

From an extensive interview he did with Campbell shortly after her appointment as Defence Minister, Peter Newman noted, "Although she empathizes with the military mind, Campbell was extremely surprised at being transferred to National Defence ..."[6] But a few practical explanations suggest themselves for her transfer. By the time of the cabinet shuffle of January 1993, it had become clear that continued high military spending and the EH101 helicopter purchase were liabilities for the Tories that were not going away and that Marcel Masse's behaviour as Defence Minister was not helping. Campbell's B.C. roots would make her better able to defend the large contracts allocated to Quebec. At the same time, Campbell's sponsorship of contracts for Quebec would allow her to shore up support in that province for her leadership ambitions. As a woman, Campbell might be a more persuasive advocate of defence spending to other women. Opinion polls generally show a significant gender gap on defence issues, with women more opposed to military programs than men.

Same Policies, Different Promotion

Campbell's short term as Defence Minister provides some clues about what she may be like as prime minister. The most contentious issue she has had to deal with has been the government's purchase of the EH101, which a March 1993 Gallup poll indicated was opposed by 69 percent of Canadians. Despite the disproportionate amount of benefits derived by the Quebec aerospace industry from the contract, an even higher percentage — 77 percent — of Quebecers opposed the deal.

In the face of this opposition, Campbell made a promise reminiscent of statements made by Brian Mulroney. In an April 1993 interview, a CBC television reporter asked her, "If you get into an election campaign and the polls show that Canadians don't share your support for this program, would you walk away from it?" Campbell responded by saying, "Well, I don't think of it in those terms. I think of doing what I think is right. And what I think is right is to continue this program."[7]

Despite all the negative commentary in letters to the editor, the resolutions against the helicopter purchase passed by municipal councils, the repeated comparisons of the allocation of $5.8 billion for helicopters and cuts to social programs, and the results of opinion polls demonstrating the contrary, Campbell insisted, "This [EH101] program is a high priority. I think Canadians understand."[8]

In defending the EH101 helicopter purchase on an April 27, 1993 CBC "Prime Time" special investigative report, Campbell gave a demonstration of her communications technique of putting issues in "personal language" so that the public will be able to understand and accept government policy:

> If you're a fisherman, fishing off the east coast, and you're out of work and you're collecting unemployment, because other countries are fishing in your water, and you don't have the naval capability to survey that, to lay charges, to enforce the agreement that we negotiated with other countries, you're going to sit there in your kitchen and you're going to say, 'Where in the heck is the Canadian navy, why aren't they there to protect me?' If you're somebody who's dealing with the problem of the drug trade, and people tell you, you know, mother ships are unloading small ships off our coast and drugs are coming into Canada, and they say 'Where the heck is the Canadian navy? Why can't we control this?' If you've lost a member of your family, if the breadwinner of your family has died in a fishing accident or a marine accident and we say the rescue helicopters couldn't take off because it was a forty knot wind and yes, helicopters exist that could have saved your husband, you're going to say, 'Why are we flying these forty-year-old helicopters? Why don't we have the capability to protect lives on our coast?'[9]

The images Campbell evokes are of ordinary people — fishermen, people trying to control illegal drugs, people in need of rescue — with critical problems that can only be solved by the EH101 purchase. But do her statements stand up to scrutiny?

Unemployment in the Atlantic fishery is not caused primarily by illegal fishing in Canada's coastal waters. A history of domestic overfishing resulting from high quotas set by the Department of Fisheries and the inability of the Canadian government to negotiate better controls on the legal fishing done by foreign countries are much stronger factors in producing unemployment in Atlantic Canada. In terms of lessening the suffering that this unemployment is causing, using the money equivalent to just six helicopters would enable the government to double the assistance that it made available to Newfoundland fishermen. When pressured to find more money, however, Fisheries Minister John Crosbie said there was no more to give.

The same faults can be found in Campbell's statements relating to controlling the illegal use of drugs. Buying EH101 helicopters to strengthen Canada's existing interdiction capability will not solve the drug problem and cannot be justified when compared to other options. The United States, with the most aggressive and well-funded drug interdiction program in the world, is able to intercept only a small percentage of the illegal drugs entering the country. Campbell would have known from her experience as Minister of Justice how minimal the impact has been of drug seizures on illegal drug consumption. *Juristat,* the government's own publication on developments in the field of justice, reported in 1990, "Although many substantial drug seizures are made, their impact on reducing the availability of illicit drugs on the Canadian market is small."[10] The report recommends that, on the basis of information derived from intelligence sources and drug seizure statistics, long-term impacts must be achieved through strategies "such as reducing demand among consumers and combatting the production of illicit substances in source countries."[11] Yet federal cuts to health care have meant that provinces have less money for addiction treatment programs. As well, the Conservatives cut $4.4 billion from the development aid budget between 1988 and 1993.

Campbell makes perhaps the strongest emotional appeal in her reference to people potentially dying in accidents if the government does not buy the EH101. She does not address the question of why Canada is the only country in the world that is going to try to use the EH101 for search and rescue, despite the helicopter's dubious appropriateness for this work. Even Britain and Italy, where the helicopters are designed and produced, have chosen other kinds of helicopters for search and rescue purposes. The United States and the Scandinavian countries, whose search and rescue teams face Arctic conditions similar to those in Canada's north, are not buying the EH101. In any case, although search and rescue is the reason used most often in public relations efforts to sell the purchase, only fifteen of the fifty EH101s Canada is buying will be devoted to that purpose.

With all of the "people-focused" arguments, Campbell backs herself into a corner. If Canada's current ability to do drug interdiction, search and rescue, and fisheries patrol is so inadequate as to endanger people's livelihood and even their lives, then Canada should be looking for "off-the-shelf" aircraft that it can purchase and operate immediately. By contracting to buy the EH101 helicopter, which is still in its testing stage, the government acknowledges that Canada will have to wait at least six years for delivery. Since military equipment design and production typically run behind schedule — and there have already been problems with the EH101 that have held up its completion — a more realistic delivery date would be after the turn of the century. In the meantime, existing helicopters, in need of overhauls and upgrading, may be run past safe limits.

Resisting Change

In deciding to buy the EH101, the Conservative government has opted to buy the most expensive military helicopter in the world in greater numbers than any other country in the world. It is worth analyzing this decision to make, at $5.8 billion, the second most expensive military purchase in Canadian history at a time when the Cold War is over and government ministers are preaching restraint. It is worth examining Campbell's willingness to jeopardize her own political popularity on a deal that she is reported to have initially opposed in cabinet.

The EH101 deal has been in the works at the Defence Department since 1986. Defence officials were looking for an anti-submarine helicopter to be carried on the navy's frigates, which the Canadian government had bought for about $9 billion. A consortium made up of the British Westland company, Agusta SpA, an

Italian state-owned corporation, and their Canadian partners promoted the EH (European Helicopter) model 101 as "the aircraft best suited for future anti-submarine warfare operations."[12] The military trade publication *Wings* extolled the virtues of the EH101, saying it would prepare Canada for "turn of the century warfare."[13] This was at a time when Canada's official defence policy stated that the threat for the foreseeable future would be the Soviet Union; with its state-of-the-art frigates and helicopters, Canada would, in the event of war, clear the Atlantic sea lanes of Soviet nuclear submarines. With the collapse of the Soviet Union, the Defence Department shifted the rationale for the EH101 acquisition but did not re-evaluate the purchase. In fact, in 1990 the department rolled an order for new search and rescue helicopters into the EH101 purchase, adding substantially to the numbers to be bought.

Campbell had a number of opportunities to get out of the EH101 deal. The spectacular turnaround in relations with the countries of the former Soviet Union eliminated the original rationale for buying the EH101 — its specialized ability to hunt and attack the sophisticated nuclear submarines of the Soviet navy. With Russian submarines mostly tied up in their home ports, the American military for their part had cancelled major anti-submarine equipment purchases. As well, by the time Campbell became Defence Minister in 1993, debates about how to reduce the deficit dominated Canadian politics. Patrick Boyer and Garth Turner, other Tory leadership hopefuls, argued the EH101 purchase should be cancelled in light of the need for fiscal restraint. A Gallup poll published in May 1993 revealed that a majority of Canadians, including a majority of people who supported the Conservative Party, wanted to see military spending cut.

The Auditor General, Denis Desautels, had provided Campbell with another attractive "out." In his 1992 report, Desautels had said that "information necessary to determine the need for search and rescue resources and alternatives for providing search and rescue services is incomplete." Commenting in general on military spending as a means of industrial development, the Auditor General warned, "We found that the costs associated with these initiatives [the six largest Defence Department capital projects] were significant and that generally they have not resulted in new industrial activity that is sustainable and competitive in domestic and world marketplaces, as required by current government policy."[14]

In addition, alarming developments with the EH101's Italian partner, Agusta SpA, argued for at least putting the contract on hold. On April 10, 1993, Italian police arrested Roberto d'Alessandro, Agusta's president, on bribery charges. This followed the arrest in February of an Agusta agent in Belgium, who was jailed as part of an inquiry into possible corruption in the sale of Agusta helicopters to the Belgian army. In February, Agusta's chief pilot as well as three other crew members died in the crash of an EH101 prototype, prompting a judicial inquiry by the Italian government. These problems compounded the unease created by bickering among the EH101's consortium partners and the fact that a bankrupt Agusta had to be taken over in 1992 by an Italian state-owned conglomerate. At a minimum, a rethinking of the number of helicopters that Canada would buy could be justified by these events. Italy had reduced its order from 36 to 16 and the British navy was committed to buying just 44. None of the 700 other orders that the consortium claimed would result in economic benefits for their Canadian partners had materialized.

Rather than seeing the opportunities to get out of the deal created by these developments, when they were raised as problems Campbell came out fighting, opting for a different "communications" technique — obfuscation. She tried to diminish the relevance of the EH101 crash and deaths in Italy by stating in the House of Commons that the prototype that had crashed was not the same one that Canada was buying. What Campbell concealed from MPs was the fact that in reaction to the EH101 crash, the Italian government grounded *all* prototypes of the aircraft because, until there was a full investigation, no one could say whether the problem with the prototype that had crashed was not a fundamental design flaw shared by all EH101s.

Campbell claimed that her "background in strategic studies" — she actually studied Soviet politics, not strategic studies — made her well aware of the diminished Russian threat but claimed that there were 900 enemy submarines in the world.[15] In fact, stripping away all non-military submarines, there are actually 700.[16] Almost 40 percent belong to the United States, NATO countries or close American allies such as Japan. William Kaufmann, strategic analyst with the Brookings Institution, expressed surprise at Canada's pursuit of an anti-submarine capability and asked in jest whether Canada now considered the United States a threat.[17] The Russians operate about another 35 percent of the world's subs, but their fleet is shrinking and largely confined to home ports.

Campbell conjured up a potential threat from Third World submarines, but none of these vessels can reach Canadian waters and each Third World country has a fleet of less than seven, on average. Justifying buying thirty-five EH101s to stave off a Third World threat implies that Canada would have to prepare for war on its own against a number of Third World countries at the same time; even at that, Canada already has aircraft that can carry out an anti-submarine function. The super-sophisticated EH101s would be "overkill" in dealing with Third World submarines that are mostly decades old and militarily obsolete. As a more effective measure to deal with potential Third World threats, Canada could consider not supplying these countries with arms. Most of the Third World countries with submarines currently purchase military goods, either directly or indirectly, from Canada.

Asked what she thought of Patrick Boyer's call for the EH101 to be cancelled in the name of fiscal restraint, Campbell snapped back that he could say what he wanted, "that's something the Prime Minister should decide. It's a free country so he can say what he wants."[18] While Campbell also talked about eliminating the national debt, her proposals involved cutting spending on social programs, not the military. Campbell argued that one of the benefits of the EH101 purchase was its job creation potential; however, spending on social programs such as housing creates five times as many jobs for the same amount of money. She tried to shield the military from the public's interest in a peace dividend, not only by fiercely defending the EH101 purchase, but by misrepresenting the overall trend in Canadian military spending. Campbell claimed in an interview that "national defence has taken huge budget cuts, beginning in 1989 and through the end of 1998."[19]

Aside from accounting changes that allowed GST and pension payments to be deducted from the military budget, Canadian military spending is about as high as it has ever been since World War II. During the decade of the 1980s, successive federal governments increased military spending by 40 percent in real terms (after accounting for inflation), increases they justified as necessary to protect Canadians from the Soviet threat.

Huge budget cuts have been announced in the 1990s, but they are cuts in the amount that the military requested, not in their actual $12 billion budget. With this curious method of accounting, Finance Minister Mazankowski was able to announce $5.9 billion in spending cuts from the military budget from 1993 to 1998, even though Canadian military spending will actually rise each year during this period. The Defence Department could ask for double its budget, receive an incremental increase, and still claim that its budget had been slashed.

Selling the EH101

Whether or not Campbell initially opposed the EH101 deal as Liberal Leader Jean Chrétien claimed in the House of Commons on February 25, 1993, by the time she became Defence Minister and a Tory leadership candidate she would have had to demonstrate a willingness to buck an extraordinarily powerful system in order to take an anti-EH101 stand.

Powerful interests in Canada support high military spending, the same interests who have led the charge against social spending. The Business Council on National Issues (BCNI), whose membership consists of the chief executive officers of the 160 largest corporations in Canada, has issued policy papers adopted almost word-for-word by the Conservative government. These papers argue the need for massive new spending on weapons systems. By 1993, the Tories had "improved" Canada's rank for military dollars spent among the largest world military spenders from fifteenth, where it was in the beginning of the 1980s, to tenth. This expansion of the military budget increased the opportunities for military industries to land lucrative government contracts.

Campbell's claim to want to change "the way we do politics in this country" would be put to the test by the EH101 purchase, because military spending, backroom lobbying and political favours are intimately bound together in Canada. Marcel Masse was one of the first cabinet ministers to provide Campbell with support in her leadership drive. In December 1992, three months before she officially declared her candidacy, Masse shepherded Campbell around Quebec, introducing her to key opinion leaders. Before the beginning of the leadership debate held in Montreal in April 1993, a Radio Canada reporter was able to break through what she described in French as a "wall of security" to find the candidate "surrounded by Brian Mulroney's key advisors and image makers." Masse was part of this inner circle.

Interviewed at the scene of the debate about his role in her campaign, Masse said in French, "Mrs. Campbell has staked a lot on the spontaneity of her organization — a lot of young people, people who have had little involvement in politics. But these people have realized that experience counts in terms of organization." It is this experience in organizing politically, particularly in Quebec, that Campbell would have risked losing by opposing Masse on the EH101 contract.

Paul Curley was another key Tory insider involved in the EH101 deal who became part of the Campbell campaign inner circle. Curley's involvement with the Conservative Party dated back to the late 1960s. He was a special assistant to Robert Stanfield between 1972 and 1974, the Conservative Party's national director from 1979 to 1981, Mulroney's campaign secretary for the 1984 election and a behind-the-scenes advisor to Marcel Masse when he was Communications Minister in the mid-1980s. According to author John Sawatsky, Curley "had more clout with Masse than some of his aides."[20] Sawatsky claims that between them, Curley and his lobbying firm partner, Pierre Fortier, "knew every Tory of consequence in the country."[21] In 1993, Curley acted as a media spokesman for Campbell and managed her campaign during the crucial week of the leadership convention.

In what *The Globe and Mail* called "an unusual move," the Defence Department hired Paul Curley's public relations firm in the summer of 1992 "to provide advice on how to present the [EH101] project to the cabinet and how to sell it to the public."[22] Defence paid Advance Planning and Communications $50,000 for six weeks of work done in the period leading up to cabinet review of the project when the whole deal looked as if it was in trouble. According to Lieutenant Karen Mair of the Defence Department, the firm designed a communications plan and advised the department how they could handle criticism of the purchase.[23]

It might come as a surprise to Canadians that a federal department can hire a politically connected public relations firm at taxpayers' expense to overcome public opposition to the expenditure of public funds on a purchase the majority of people reject. Defence already has 95 people on staff working to present the department to the public in the best possible light. But Lieutenant Mair insisted that there was nothing wrong with Curley's firm getting the contract, for it gave the department an "outside" perspective on what was happening. For his part, Curley claimed that he had never talked to any cabinet minister about the purchase, although he admitted his Tory connections had not hurt his firm in getting the job.[24]

While the taxpayer paid for the work that Advance Planning and Communications did, the results of that work are available to the public only in heavily censored form. Canada's feeble Access to Information Act allows the government to censor any "advice or recommendations developed by or for a government institution or a Minister of the Crown." Even the table of contents of the "Communications Plan" and the signatures of the Advanced Planning senior partner in correspondence with Defence officials were censored under the terms of the Act. What the released portions of the firm's communications strategy did reveal, however, is that a key objective was to gain "recognition of the acquisition as an investment of government and nationwide dimensions instead of a narrow self indulgence by one particular department."[25]

The strategists also identified as a particular problem the criticisms of the helicopter purchase appearing in *The Globe and Mail*. To combat these criticisms, the plan included promotion of a number of "unbiased" sources for media comment. These sources, who were subsequently extensively quoted by the media, included people such as Alex Morrison of the Canadian Institute of Strategic Studies, which got $105,000 in funding from the Defence Department in 1992 and receives financial backing from Canadian Marconi Co., one of the EH101 contractors. The plan also recommended in aggressive terms that measures be taken to "anticipate and effectively neutralize EH101-specific criticisms."[26]

Paul Curley has a history of helping out prominent Tory politicians at critical times in their careers. One writer observed that "Curley holds more IOUs than a finance company."[27] These IOUs undoubtedly contribute to Curley's status as one of the most effective Tory lobbyists working in Ottawa. Curley now held even more IOUs from Campbell for his work on her leadership campaign. And these were IOUs from a prime minister — at least temporarily.

The public relations efforts Advance Planning did for Defence were only the tip of the iceberg in the campaign to sell the EH101. Paramax, the electronics company that held a contract to supply parts for the EH101, covered its bets by hiring more than one lobbying firm connected directly to cabinet ministers and Prime Minister Brian Mulroney. One of these firms was Temple-Scott, headed by Ian Anderson, who had worked in the prime minister's office until 1987 as Mulroney's deputy principal secretary. Anderson, one of many who peddled his connections with Mulroney, was also on Campbell's team.

Another lobbying firm employed by Paramax was the Government Business Consulting Group. The key person working for Paramax from this firm was Fred Doucet, former chief of staff to Mulroney and one of his closest friends stretching back to his college days at St. Francis Xavier. Doucet had been an organizer for Mulroney in his successful bid to unseat Joe Clark as Tory leader. Mulroney once said that he could ask Doucet to move a skyscraper two inches and by the next morning, Doucet would have found a way of doing it.[28]

When questioned a week before the EH101 acquisition went before cabinet for review, Brian Mulroney said he did not have "the foggiest idea" what it was for. It may seem incomprehensible that the prime minister would not know what the second largest purchase in Canadian history was about shortly before he decided to go ahead with it, but the Curley, Anderson and Doucet connections begin to explain how the deal got through, to the surprise of even those supervising the EH101 project within Defence. Lobbyists are often offered an extra incentive to push for a contract, sometimes in the form of a generous monthly retainer for a one- to three-year period if the contract is successfully landed.

But Curley, Anderson and Doucet were not the only lobbyists involved. There were 250 other firms besides Paramax who stood to benefit from the EH101 acquisition, and a number of these hired their own lobbyists. For example, General Electric Canada and Computing Devices Co. both hired the mammoth lobbying firm, Hill and Knowlton Canada, to represent their interests. Two Hill and Knowlton consultants, Bruce McLellan and Greg Lyle, were involved in Campbell's campaign. Canadian Marconi Co. hired Corporation House, one of the oldest public relations firms in Canada. Litton Systems Canada hired William Neville and Associates. Bill Neville, known for his high-profile work for the tobacco industry, was chief of staff to Joe Clark when he was prime minister, supervised Mulroney's transition team after the 1984 election, and was regularly consulted by Mulroney subsequently. Neville, whom Sawatsky calls "the ultimate insider,"[29] was also involved in Campbell's leadership campaign.

The hired lobbyists and the in-house public relations representatives of the EH101 contractors not only approached cabinet ministers, but they also sought out backbench MPs to promote the deal's economic benefits for particular regions. As well, they did extensive work to get the media on side, including briefings organized across the country for editorial writers on the advantages of the EH101.

Perhaps the strongest lobbying card that Paramax had to play was the fact that it had Paul Manson on its team. Manson had joined the Canadian air force in 1952 and eventually rose through the ranks to the top of the Canadian military, holding the position of Chief of the Defence Staff between 1986 and 1989. In the late seventies, Manson had been program manager within the Defence Department for the CF18 fighter plane acquisition. At a total cost of $5.2 billion, this purchase is the third largest ever made by the Canadian government. In the 1980s, Manson had been involved in determining the specifications the military demanded for the helicopters it would buy, specifications that it turned out could be met only by the EH101.

As soon as Manson retired in 1989, he began working for Unisys Corp., the parent company of Paramax. His stint at the Unisys head office allowed Manson to keep to the letter of the civil service post-employment code guidelines that discourage direct lobbying within the year following a top civil servant's release from government. With this formality over with, Paramax appointed him their senior vice-president in 1990 and promoted him to president in 1992, the year of the most intense lobbying over the EH101 purchase.

Between 1983 and 1993, Paramax hired between fifty and seventy-five former staff members from the Defence Department, a practice common in Canada's military industry. One concern with this practice is that these employees will have preferential access to their former colleagues in Defence to influence purchasing recommendations. A more fundamental problem is that with the career pattern of most of Canada's top military officers extending into civilian jobs that are dependent on continued high spending on procurement, there is a built-in incentive for these officers to recommend a national defence policy based on this kind of spending. The long periods involved in weapons procurements can exceed the time that the officers recommending them have left to serve with the armed forces, so they can recommend projects that may benefit the corporations they ultimately will work for once they have retired from the military.

Manson is not one of those former Defence personnel who have recognized the ethical difficulties inherent in this situation. Commenting on the connections between the Defence Department and the military industry, Manson has said, "It's part of a continuum. There's a perfect consistency in the military and the industrial sides of the program. I feel privileged, and I feel that I'm serving my country."[30]

The issue of Defence staff being hired by industry came to the fore in 1986 when Oerlikon Aerospace hired the four Defence officials who had been the project managers for a $1.1 billion contract Oerlikon had received the same year. In response, Ed Healey, Assistant Deputy Minister of Defence (Matériel), said that the department would do what it could in future to ensure that the relationship between the industry and government was kept proper. But in 1990, Healey himself joined the Ottawa lobbying firm, CFN Consultants, where he has worked on the EH101 contract.

With all these forces in play, as well as the political motive of spending defence dollars in particular regions, a tendency can develop to proceed with the most expensive rather than the least expensive of the options available to the Defence Department. In the course of arranging the EH101 acquisition, the department increased the numbers to be acquired and, in the words of one contractor, "thwarted"[31] attempts by helicopter suppliers who proposed cheaper ways to fill the department's needs.

Campbell played along with her department's strategy to deny that there was any option other than to buy fifty EH101s. In a March 13, 1993 article in the Vancouver *Province,* she vigorously attacked the NDP's proposal that Canada follow the low-cost solution the Americans had pursued to fill their search and rescue needs: upgrading their existing fleet of Boeing helicopters. Boeing had said that, based on its experience upgrading the American search and rescue aircraft, it could put new engines, drive trains, de-icing equipment and a range of other improvements into Canada's thirteen Labrador helicopters for a total cost of about $130 million.

In her attack on the Boeing option, Campbell said that the upgrades would last for no more than five years. Boeing representatives had said that they would last for fifteen, especially since

Canada's Labradors had accumulated relatively few flight hours. In the Toronto leadership debate, Campbell exaggerated the age of the helicopters by calling them forty-year-old machines, even though they were acquired in 1963. Boeing argues that aircraft should not be evaluated in terms of their age, like the family car; the integrity of helicopter airframes can be extended indefinitely if they are given a high standard of maintenance, which has been done with the Canadian Labradors. Campbell refers to the death of a Labrador crew member in a 1992 crash near Bella Coola, B.C., as evidence that the EH101 would save lives. But Boeing can cite the Labrador's almost flawless accident record in Canada. As well, company representatives have repeatedly pleaded with the Canadian government — to no avail — to upgrade its helicopters to standard, as all other countries owning these models have.

Before the pressure began to mount in the Defence Department to get the EH101 helicopter, pilots were pleased with the Labradors. A 1982 Defence Department document, "Report on an Evaluation of Search and Rescue," contained very positive pilot statements on the Labrador's advantages. While the EH101 may have certain technical advantages, concerns exist about the power of the downdraft from its rotors and problems with visibility. Paramax claims that the downdraft problem can be solved if pilots fly in at the right altitude and hover at the right height, but this may not be easy to do under the rough conditions that can plague search and rescue operations. Campbell has said that "logic compels a decision to buy new," but in buying new helicopters that have not had their flaws worked out, Canada is actually taking a very expensive risk. New aircraft, particularly ones equipped with complex electronics, typically go way over budget and over schedule; the British EH101 is already two years behind schedule. Pilots have to be retrained to fly new aircraft, at considerable expense.

Campbell claims that upgrading rather than buying new EH101s would not save much money, even while Boeing points to its contract with the American military as proof that it can deliver on its offer of providing upgraded helicopters at $9.96 million each. Campbell also rejects the option of buying new Sea King helicopters from Sikorsky, even though this is the route that the British government has taken to meet its search and rescue needs, at half the cost of the EH101.[32]

Staying the Course

In all her statements about the EH101, Campbell departs very little
from the script written by Advance Planning and Communications. In a speech she made in Sarnia in April 1993, she seemed
to waver when asked whether all fifty EH101s were required, but
by the next week she was back on track, arguing that cutting back
from fifty would save an insignificant amount of money. With
advisors in her leadership campaign like Masse, Curley and
Neville who are closely connected with the EH101 purchase,
Campbell's "stay the course" approach on this issue is perhaps
predictable.

However, the "politics of inclusion" have fared badly in her
handling of the issue. Campbell does not meet with groups opposed to the EH101 purchase, such as the Canadian Peace Alliance (CPA), a coalition of peace and environmental groups. In
1990, the CPA had organized a cross-Canada inquiry, with a panel
of members from the three major political parties hearing a total
of about 600 briefs from Canadians on what they thought Canada's new security priorities should be. CPA tried to get an appointment to see Campbell to report the results of this inquiry and
to discuss the helicopter issue from the day her appointment as
Defence Minister was announced. Unlike previous Tory Defence
Ministers — including Perrin Beatty and Bill McKnight — Campbell never could find time to meet with CPA representatives,
despite repeated requests.

Instead of opening the door to those who do not have the insider
connections of the EH101 partners, Campbell allowed more of the
EH101 contracts to be awarded after she became Defence Minister
in an attempt to ensure that no future government could afford to
get out of the deal. Every new contract signed increased the penalties that would be incurred by the deal's cancellation; Liberal
Party researchers estimated the cost of these penalties to be over
$300 million.

The significance of Campbell's decision to "stay the course on
the helicopter deal" means that high defence spending will be
locked in for the foreseeable future. In an article entitled "Business
as Usual for the Military," *Globe and Mail* reporter Geoffrey York
observed: "The helicopter contract is expected to consume about
10 per cent of the defence procurement budget over the next 13

years. If the department was expecting a significant decline in its $12.5 billion budget, it would be unable to afford the new EH101 helicopters ..."[33]

In the light of Campbell's refusal to meet with groups opposed to the EH101, and of the impact of the EH101 purchase in locking in high military spending for the foreseeable future, Campbell's following statements ring rather hollow: "And if Canadians then say, look, 8 percent of our budget on national defence is too much, then we look within that to set priorities ... And that's what I'd like to do; involve Canadians in setting those priorities, because they have to live with the result. It's too important to deal with behind closed doors."[34]

Somalia: Peacekeeping Comes Unstuck

The issue of the purchase of the EH101 helicopters raises serious questions about the priorities of the Canadian military and how they are determined. Do Canadians get the opportunity to have any say in what their armed forces should be doing in the post-Cold War era? Would they choose, for example, to place more emphasis on peacekeeping than on war preparation, given that the enemy we spent four decades preparing for has disappeared? Polls suggest that Canadians expect a peace dividend from the end of the Cold War and that they are strongly supportive of continuing Canada's peacekeeping role. But the "politics of inclusion" apparently do not extend to input from ordinary Canadians on matters of the military and where the armed forces should be focusing their resources.

Military policy in Canada has been driven, since the mid-1980s at least, by a shift in emphasis to expensive, high-tech military equipment and away from personnel. It seems driven, considering the nature of the helicopter purchase and the lobbying that led to it, by the logic and the political requirements of the military-industrial alliance that has been fostered by the government. In the absence of effective and meaningful conflict-of-interest legislation governing retired military men, this trend is almost certain to continue.

Yet this reality did not stop the Mulroney government and Campbell from using the positive images of Canadian peacekeepers for their own political purposes: for example, the use of videos of peacekeeping operations during the constitutional referendum by the Yes side. The peacekeeping portion of the Defence Department budget has never exceeded 4.8 percent.

In a front page article on May 27, 1993, *The Globe and Mail*'s European correspondent Paul Koring interviewed "officers serving in Bosnia and officials who travelled with External Affairs Minister Barbara McDougall" on her trip to the former Yugoslavia. The article detailed just how desperate the army was in attempting to meet its overseas commitments of 4,500 soldiers in a dozen missions around the world. And the situation promises to get worse, as Defence Department plans will see the number of army battalions reduced even further by early 1994.

Campbell is aware of this and yet has not responded to the growing crisis in peacekeeping and peacemaking. Instead, she has attempted to justify the high-cost, high-tech direction of the military by suggesting that Canada's peacekeeping role might, in the future, be met with the military's newly acquired hardware rather than troops. When describing the cuts she is planning to make — including 5,000 more soldiers and civilian personnel — she reemphasized her commitment to the EH101s. "There is, however, one project which is essential to the modernization program that will not be deferred"[35] — the fifty EH101s.

Commenting on the difficulty in meeting Canada's peacekeeping commitments, Campbell stated: "Our forces are pretty much stretched in terms of providing ground forces for peacekeeping. On the other hand, there is a role for the navy, there is a role for the air force in some areas of peacekeeping." In short, Canada's effectiveness in peacekeeping will be determined by its procurement program, not by a reconsideration of the cuts to army personnel — or of the number of EH101s the government is committed to. Yet, as Paul Koring pointed out, the UN "has a surfeit of NATO vessels enforcing a blockade, while the United Nations is desperately seeking additional ground troops to protect besieged Bosnian Muslim enclaves."[36] Lieutenant-General Gordon Reay, while emphasizing that he is committed to whatever policy the government decides upon, stated: "We can do it [missions in Bosnia and Somalia], but as we continue to shrink ... there's a price that has to be paid." That price, said General Reay, is capability.

Campbell's commitment to peacekeeping consistently plays second fiddle to her commitment to the helicopters and her department's military procurement ideology. The cuts to personnel have already devastated some communities in the country, particularly in the Atlantic region. People living near Canadian Forces Base Cornwallis in Nova Scotia have attempted to fight the closing of that base by proposing that it be developed into a training centre for UN peacekeeping forces.

In a style that has come to characterize Campbell's approach to citizens' groups of any kind, Campbell ridiculed the committee's suggestion of a UN peacekeeping training centre: "[It's] a wonderful idea for most people who do not know anything about peacekeeping."[37] Yet the idea has the support of Sir Brian Urquhart, former Assistant Secretary-General at the UN and the official responsible for establishing most of the UN's peacekeeping missions, and Canadian Brigadier-General Clayton Beattie, commander of the peacekeeping force in Cyprus during the fighting on the island and later involved in the UN mission in Cambodia. Urquhart, Beattie and others with decades of experience at senior command levels of UN peacekeeping had written in support of the idea of establishing a peacekeeping training centre at CFB Cornwallis. In fact, Beattie had helped write the 1992 report "CFB Cornwallis: A Blueprint for a Peacekeeping Training Centre of Excellence." This report, prepared in consultation with former UN commanders and UN officials, provided a curriculum for training peacekeeping officers and troops.

Campbell's tendency to "shoot from the lip" had got her in trouble once again. The Nova Scotia Conservative premier, Donald Cameron, had actively promoted the Cornwallis proposal and all three parties had endorsed it in the provincial legislature.

Campbell's sole basis for making such a strong condemnation of the concept of a peacekeeping training centre was, in her words, "discussions with senior members of the Canadian military who are a bit perplexed as to what you would teach people but the normal skills of a good combat-ready military."[38] If she had stopped to seek other advice before making such a categorical statement, she would have found that in 1991 Canada had co-sponsored a UN resolution calling for the establishment of such a centre.

Canadian troops currently receive a maximum of two weeks' special preparation for peacekeeping. Canadian military training has not changed significantly from the days of the Cold War, when preparations centred on fighting a high-intensity, highly mobile ground war in Europe focused on rapidly capturing the most territory possible. It stands to reason that a military trained to be "combat-ready" for such a role has not received the best preparation to be peacekeepers.

Murder at Belet Huen

As if the need for training in peacekeeping were not already obvious it became so, ironically and tragically, less than a month after Campbell ridiculed the idea. A Somali prisoner being held in custody by Canadians who had captured him as he tried to enter their compound was tortured and beaten to death on March 16, 1993, by Canadian soldiers. Five soldiers were eventually arrested and charged. One of the soldiers, a Métis from Saskatchewan, allegedly attempted suicide after being arrested. His family vigorously denied the claim, saying that he, too, had been beaten. And in an earlier incident, on March 4, two other Somalis were shot, one fatally, by Canadian soldiers. That death turned out to be highly suspicious as well. The military surgeon attending the two Somalis revealed that the dead man had been shot in the back and the head as he lay wounded on the ground.

Canadians did not learn of the March 16 incident until over two weeks later — March 31. On April 29, a month after military officials informed reporters that the death "appeared to be a serious homicide case," Campbell announced an inquiry into the incident.[39] But on the same day new questions were being asked about why it had taken so long for Canadians to learn about the incident — and the questions involved Campbell.

Campbell claimed that she had learned only of the death of a Somali on March 17 and that "it was not until March 31 that ... the death had now been characterized as a homicide or as a murder."[40] But she was immediately contradicted by her chief of staff, Admiral John Anderson. "The minister has acknowledged that she knew on March 19 we were deploying a police investigation team to Somalia."[41] Campbell's claim that she only learned of a death and not a suspicious death was directly contradicted by her most senior official.

Campbell never adequately addressed the contradictions between her chief of staff's explanation of the events and her own and was criticized by opposition parties for being absent from the House of Commons during much of the time that followed the revelations. For a good part of April, Campbell was on the campaign trail, away from the tough questions of opposition members.

The day that Campbell announced an inquiry into the death at Belet Huen she was accused of attempting to cover up her role in the events surrounding the delayed announcement of the killing. The inquiry would be closed to the public, said Campbell, to ensure that witnesses would give candid evidence. Yet she could have declared the inquiry open. Campbell did break with tradition, however, by appointing two civilians to the board of inquiry. One of the civilians was Harriet Critchley, the Director of Strategic Studies at the University of Calgary, who is well known within disarmament circles for her stalwart support of the Canadian military.

Ironically, given Campbell's hostility to the suggestion of special training for peacekeepers, the mandate of the inquiry focused precisely on this and related issues. The inquiry was to examine the Canadian Airborne Regiment and its battle group. It would look into "the general question of discipline and the general question of preparation — and the ethos and values that surround the performance of people's duties in the field."[42] It would also examine the Airborne's "leadership, training, selection, professional values and the extent to which cultural differences affected the conduct of operations."[43]

Had the military brass not resisted the proposals for peacekeeping training — a resistance reinforced by Campbell — it is possible that the decision to send the highly aggressive Airborne Regiment might not have been made. And it soon became clear that it was not simply the lack of technical training that the Defence Department was concerned about.

Rumours of racism among many of the Regiment's members were confirmed when one of the soldiers sent to Somalia, Corporal Matt McKay, was identified as a member of a neo-Nazi group and a photograph of him wearing an Adolf Hitler T-shirt surfaced in the press. The photo was apparently taken in his military barracks. The Canadian Jewish Congress issued a statement claiming that as many as twenty-four Canadian soldiers serving in Somalia had neo-Nazi connections.[44]

While government House leader Harvie Andre tried to downplay the issue, stating that soldiers could attend meetings of any group they chose in their off-duty hours, Campbell moved quickly to address the question of racists in the military. "In my opinion it is not acceptable. We have not ... deliberately asked people about their memberships. I am instituting a review of our recruiting policy to ensure that is done."[45]

Clearly, Campbell cannot be blamed for the fact that the armed forces harbour racists in their ranks. She was only appointed Defence Minister in January 1993. Yet her handling of the events in Somalia, the restricted terms of reference of the inquiry and the fact that it will not be able to investigate her role in the attempts to cover up the incidents confirm that Campbell's politics, far from being "fresh and new," are part of politics as usual in Ottawa.

While Campbell deserves some credit for examining recruiting measures to screen out racists, this is scarcely a radical approach and looks good primarily in contrast to the comments of her colleague, Harvie Andre. The inquiry, alleged the opposition in the House of Commons, was designed to get the issue off Campbell's plate until after the leadership convention — which it did. It was scheduled to report in July. And it was not just politicians who expressed this criticism. Peacekeeping hero General Lewis MacKenzie suggested that the inquiry "had to be held from the point of view of a person who is deep in the middle of a political battle and has to find some way to deflect and delay."[46]

Marketing Kim Campbell

When Brian Mulroney met in early December 1992 with his Quebec lieutenant Marcel Masse, the ostensible reason was to discuss Masse's desire to quit the cabinet. But the prime minister had one more task for his patronage boss in *la belle province*. Mulroney wanted Masse, who knew every political operative and business Tory in the province personally, to introduce his candidate of choice to the people who count in Quebec. Mulroney asked Masse to take on the task of chaperoning Campbell around Quebec and organizing a few private dinners to introduce her to key business people, journalists, artists and other opinion makers. Masse agreed. And Campbell's silent run for the leadership was underway.

When Mulroney won the leadership of the Conservative Party in 1983, his principal claim to being the right man for the time was based on history. It showed, argued Mulroney, that the Tories could not hope to win a majority in Canada without winning Quebec. It was the Liberal stranglehold on Quebec that had relegated the Conservatives to the role of perpetual opposition. Mulroney promised to end that era in history and he did. How he did it and how he might preserve his historic accomplishment were very much on Mulroney's mind that December day.

Many Canadian observers, politicians and otherwise, had already identified Campbell as the best bet for reviving Tory hopes. If she were to succeed, however, she would have to retain and rebuild the loose coalition of Conservative Quebec nationalists and provincial Liberals that Mulroney, the master deal-maker, had put together going into the 1984 election. Masse was the key to that coalition, which was beginning to show signs of serious wear. Mulroney knew what many commentators had observed about Quebec. In national elections, Quebecers go with the perceived winners in order to get as much as possible from Ottawa. The mantle of perceived winner was still up for grabs. Though the Tory coalition had lost many members to the Bloc Québécois, a new Tory leader carrying the promise of support outside Quebec had the potential for reversing that trend.

And so, at a time when Canadians were still wondering whether Brian Mulroney would really resign, the man himself was already preparing Campbell for the crown and offering her the entire palace entourage. Masse would not only organize a series of private dinners for Campbell, but he would bring with him to Campbell's side the entire organizing team that had helped Mulroney win the leadership of the Tory party.

The Early Weeks

At first it seemed that nothing would stop Campbell from sweeping the Tory leadership and then the country. When Mulroney finally announced his resignation on February 24, later than most analysts and Tories had expected, the sigh of relief from across the country was almost audible. But no one was prepared for one of the results of Mulroney's long-awaited departure. A poll taken a week later stunned observers and Tories alike. It showed that if Campbell were leading the Conservative Party, they would win the next election. There was the ritual muttering about it being a momentary flash, but the numbers were staggering and, given the perception that Mulroney was hated for his party's policies, almost unbelievable. A *Globe and Mail*/ComQuest poll was the first off the mark and showed a Campbell Conservative Party winning 45 percent of the vote compared to 32 percent for the Liberals and 9 percent for the NDP.[1] The attention lavished on Campbell fed on itself as each poll seemed to reinforce the last. An Angus Reid poll taken at about the same time showed similar results: Campbell Tories would get 43 percent, Chrétien Liberals 25 percent and the NDP 11 percent.[2] A Gallup poll taken after the other two was even more dramatic, and caused panic among many Liberal supporters and organizers. It showed Campbell at 50 percent compared to the Liberals at 29 percent and the NDP at 9 percent.[3]

The impact of the polls on the Conservative Party and its long-anticipated leadership race was dramatic. The Campbell juggernaut was out of control, rolling over all the plans and expectations of the prime minister, Tory members and other Tory candidates.

It was conventional wisdom that a campaign without something close to a million dollars in the kitty would not win the Tory leadership. Several Tory hopefuls had a pretty good shot at that much financial support and had been talking quietly to supporters for months, in the belief that there was no need to rush things. Michael Wilson, Barbara McDougall, Perrin Beatty, Don Mazankowski, Jean Charest and others were all considered credible candidates with serious support in the caucus and in the party.

But by the middle of March 1993, a rising tide had swept over all the conventional wisdom. And it left the contenders staggering like punch-drunk boxers. They had been beaten silly by what passed for, in these days of political cynicism, Campbellmania. Before anyone could even grasp what was happening, before the candidates' advisors and friends could talk to party members or even caucus members, the race was over for several of the heavy hitters.

Michael Wilson, obviously shell-shocked and not a little angry at the defection of his Bay Street buddies, was the first to withdraw in March. He stated that he simply could not expect to raise the money he would need to run a campaign. He was quickly followed by others who had been planning to run for years. Barbara McDougall, a minister much more senior than Campbell who had been touted for several years as the most likely woman candidate, bowed out. Then it was Bernard Valcourt and, on the same day, Perrin Beatty. Beatty, who had been working towards the leadership the longest of anyone, slipped quietly into obscurity with the statement that "an unprecedented consensus" had formed in the party and that he agreed with it.[4]

By March, Jean Charest was reportedly no longer planning to run, while Don Mazankowski was now being pressured to reconsider his decision to stay out. Only last-minute pressure from Mulroney and subtle behind-the-scenes manoeuvring in Quebec to ensure that at least some money would flow his way ultimately persuaded Charest to enter the race. But it was a testament to the remaining volatility in Canadian politics that a party so accustomed to maintaining tight control of internal developments would lose control of a situation whose outcome would determine its future.

There was a sigh of relief from the prime minister's office when Charest agreed to run, for one of the principal benefits of a leadership race was the excitement generated by the cut and thrust of the battle for the crown. For days, Campbell's enormous lead in the polls was being referred to as the evidence of a coronation.

And coronations are dull. But even with Charest's announcement, the media could not imagine anyone but Campbell winning.

Campbell, who had been acting coy for weeks, finally did the obvious. On March 24, she flew back to British Columbia, where the next morning she announced her candidacy in the presence of what one journalist cynically described as over a thousand "close personal friends."[5] Her announcement speech set the tone for the weeks of campaigning that followed and was characterized by doses of rhetoric designed to persuade the audience that Campbell would be a true democrat: She was consultative, inclusive and ready to change the political culture.

Later, Campbell held a short news conference. Her most memorable line revealed the image she wanted to create. When asked why she wanted to be prime minister, she replied: "I want to change the way people think about politics in this country by changing the way we do politics in this country." [6] Some observers thought the response was too slick and scripted. The rest of Campbell's performance was much the same — strong on image-building and rhetoric, but shallow in terms of substance.

Her delivery was designed to make Campbell seem "new and fresh," to suggest that she had not been a part of the old-style politics. It had a good spin to it, but it was all a bit too much. It was as if her handlers had coached her on the approach and given her some lines and phrases to use as examples, but were unable to teach her how to internalize the image. When asked specific questions at the news conference, she offered vague replies: "I have my own, I think, unique style of politics ... I think I have a very unique political style that is collegial and open and patient and I think it works ... When I talk about reaching out in meaningful consultation, it's something I've done ... And what we did is reached out and invited people to be part of the solution ... in fact I gave a very good speech in Toronto which was recorded on cable television and played there, so it exists in the public record."

The single strongest message was clearly focused on neutralizing the greatest liability — being a Mulroney Tory. "I think, you know, part of being, of inclusiveness in government, means reaching out and talking to people in a way that's real to them." And two minutes later: "What I want to do in our party is to reach out and make it as broadly based as possible ... I'd like to see us virtually re-invent government."[7]

Campbell gave the first major interview of her official campaign the evening of March 25 on CBC "Prime Time News." It was not a good performance and the next day reports were leaking out that her campaign staff were concerned. They should have been. Campbell was already showing signs that she was not as quick on her feet as everyone had expected. The judgement she showed in her interview with two of the country's most prominent journalists revealed that Campbell had major problems. Pamela Wallin and Peter Mansbridge had already zeroed in on Campbell's use of the phrase "inclusiveness" earlier that morning. They challenged her on her statement that she wanted to change the way politics is done. "What does it really mean?" asked Mansbridge. Campbell responded: "Well, what I think we need to do is to close the distance between people and government ... I've tried very much to do that, to reach out and broaden the base of consultation ... " Mansbridge pressed her again: "What kind of [consultation] are you talking about?" Campbell eventually explained that she wanted to change the way government communicated what it was doing. She did not intend to change policies on the basis of what people had to say to government. It was a matter of doing a better selling job. "I think we spend a ton of money on communication that does very little to make government comprehensible to Canadians. So I want to look at that whole question and devices for bringing people closer [to government]."

Mansbridge and Wallin continued to press Campbell on what made her different from Brian Mulroney. "One of [the things I want to talk about] is the way we communicate with people, the way that we focus on the people-oriented, the people focus, I guess of policy ... I think what we have to do is pull the agenda down to be much more people-oriented. That will give Canadians confidence that the goals of our policies are people goals."

The "Prime Time" team became more specific. The Conservatives had proposed a national day care program in the 1988 election and almost immediately afterwards cancelled it, but now as Defence Minister, Mansbridge reminded Campbell, she was planning to spend $5 or $6 billion on helicopters. "Is that money well spent?" What followed was five refusals by Campbell to answer the question of what she would do as prime minister if faced with buying the helicopters or putting the money into day care. It was not just impressive stonewalling; it was a remarkable contradiction of her claim to want to do politics differently. Refusing to move from her predetermined script, Campbell steadfastly defended the helicopters by referring to catching drug smugglers, saving the fishery from European overfishing, the need for environmental surveillance and the importance of saving lives. Frustrated with Campbell's refusal to answer, Wallin insisted: "If it's helicopters or day care, where do you come down?"

Campbell: "Well, why don't we say, is it search and rescue or day care?"

Wallin (getting a little testy): "Phrase it however you want, what's the answer?"

Campbell still refused to answer the question. She ended by reinforcing Wallin's point — that "leadership is about tough choices." Said Campbell: "Those are the hard choices we make in this society ... "[8] Yet she refused to make the choice. Clearly tense and angered at the persistent questioning, Campbell blew her first big opportunity to impress the public and the potential delegates to the Tory convention.

Campbell's Leadership Team

On the heels of that poor performance on the country's most prestigious news show, the country's only national newspaper suddenly turned on Campbell's tendency to flimflam. In its editorial the next morning, *The Globe* was less than kind. Pointing out that Campbell had disclosed virtually nothing about her views on the major problems facing the country and that her record was "decidedly mixed," it took particular aim at her claim to be new and fresh. "A fresh face? A new approach to politics? In her corner one finds such haggard devotees of politics-as-usual as Norm Atkins, Larry Grossman, Bill Neville, and Pat Kinsella. Even Dalton Camp shows up writing fawning newspaper columns in her praise."[9] Having climbed beyond all the other main contenders, Campbell seemed suddenly to have reached a plateau.

It had been on the advice of public relations experts like these that Campbell had delayed the announcement of her leadership bid for several weeks. She denied that she was "playing coy" and stated that she wanted to be in her home constituency, with her friends and supporters, to formally announce her candidacy. But even this seemed to be part of a highly calculated and carefully executed plan. By March 26, she was in Quebec — the part of the country most important in her plan to become prime minister.

The media were already aware of Campbell's early connections to the Mulroney mafia in Quebec. Word had leaked out about Mulroney's special assignment for Marcel Masse. Now it was reported that Masse and Treasury Board President Gilles Loiselle, another heavy hitter in the Quebec Tory machine, were engaged in a "furious backroom campaign ... to line up support from Ministers, MPs and party members. [Campbell's] intention is to reduce the status of Quebec-based Jean Charest from that of a serious contender to that of a favourite son."[10] Senate leader Guy Charbonneau, another close Mulroney loyalist and Tory bagman, was also working for Campbell, giving his extensive list of financial backers to the Campbell campaign. Campbell's campaign in Quebec was described variously as "aggressive" and "furious," with plenty of "arm twisting"[11] and the hard sell.

Veteran CBC radio reporter Jason Moscovitz was there for Campbell's arrival in Quebec. "All the organizers in the room were all of Mulroney's organizers in 1983, the ones responsible for all the dirty tricks in that campaign."[12] The continuity was eerie. As Moscovitz pulled up to the address in east-end Montreal that he had been given for Campbell's Quebec headquarters, he realized that it was the same three-storey office building that Mulroney had used. And the crowning touch was Jean-Yves Lortie, a key operative in Mulroney's campaign. His notoriety in 1983 led, according to Moscovitz, to the practice of placing reporters who came for interviews with Mulroney in a waiting room until Lortie could be hidden away. This day, March 26, ten years later, it was Lortie, dressed in a blue suit, who opened Kim Campbell's car door and was the first one to welcome her to Tory Quebec.

That Campbell would place herself in the hands of the likes of Lortie, Charbonneau, Loiselle and the others — what amounted to the entire Mulroney team from 1983 — made a mockery of her claim to be fresh and new and to have a "unique approach to politics." It also raised questions about her commitment to internal party democracy, something these men were best known for violating. Above all, it raised questions about her political judgement and her independence.

Much has been written about Jean-Yves Lortie and the other men who were in the room with Campbell when she launched the Quebec stage of her campaign. As John Sawatsky details in *The Politics of Ambition,* Lortie was a key player in the sabotage of Joe Clark's leadership in Quebec. Lortie worked closely with

Rodrigue Pageau, the man who was supposed to be Clark's chief Quebec organizer, but who in fact was a double-agent working for Mulroney. Pageau was responsible for getting pro-Clark delegates elected at constituency meetings for the upcoming leadership review. "While piously assuring Ottawa that Clark supporters were being selected ... Pageau had in fact made sure that a majority of Quebec's delegates were pro-review."[13]

Sawatsky describes Lortie as being "renowned within party circles, especially in the east end of Montreal, as a machine-style ward-healer of the old school. People would later call him 'the French poodle' because of his frizzy hair, fur coats, and penchant for gaudy jewellery ... When recruiting delegates at the grassroots level, Lortie could be heavy-handed when the need arose." One of Lortie's favourite tricks was to closet delegates away from conventions until just before a crucial vote and then bring them *en masse* to the convention floor. He did this at the leadership review meeting — busing 112 Quebec delegates to the convention arena so they could vote against Clark. "Lortie never camouflaged his true colours and later bragged about his exploits to *The Toronto Star*." Lortie, whom Sawatsky refers to as "infamous," also worked on a committee that was to seize control of the Quebec executive of the party in order to control the delegate selection process. Sawatsky suggests that Lortie was a willing player in the sabotage of Joe Clark largely because "Clark had failed them on patronage."[14]

Most of the key players in Mulroney's backroom campaign for the Tory leadership (except Pageau, who is dead) were on side with Campbell. Among them were the following:

Frank Moores: The former Newfoundland premier and founder of Government Consultants International was, according to Sawatsky, the "godfather of all the Ottawa plotting" for Mulroney. Though he had nothing against Clark, he took on the job of helping dump him with great enthusiasm as repayment to Mulroney for lucrative contracts given his consulting firm. He spent most of 1982 "working on disgruntled caucus members ... collecting money and fomenting discontent in the grassroots ..."[15] Moores later switched to Charest's campaign.

Guy Charbonneau: The Tories' fund raiser in Quebec since the 1950s, he was Mulroney's principal bagman in Quebec and a key fundraiser for Lortie and Pageau in their efforts to undermine Clark. A senator, he was also a key player in the dirty-tricks takeover of the Quebec Conservative Party executive before the 1982 leadership review.

Peter White: A business associate of Conrad Black, White was a loyal Mulroney organizer going back to Mulroney's first leadership bid in 1978 and played a key co-ordinating and administrative role for Mulroney in the approach to the leadership review and through to his successful campaign in 1983. He also had a major role in the dump-Diefenbaker movement. More recently, as an Ottawa insider and Mulroney's principal secretary, he has been implicated in the dealings that led the prime minister's office to overrule government civil servants and provide Curragh Resources with generous federal grants to start up the ill-fated Westray Mine.

Bill Neville: Despite having served for a long time as Joe Clark's chief of staff and right-hand man, Neville proved willing to advise Mulroney on his leadership bid behind Clark's back at a critical stage in the process. Neville ended up as senior Mulroney advisor and image-maker. A consultant/lobbyist *par excellence,* he is yet another Tory insider who rents out his political influence through his firm Neville and Associates.

The backroom boys associated with Mulroney's rise to power were by no means the only political operators eager to flock to Campbell's campaign. Excited by the prospect of remaining in power with access to government influence and largesse, dozens of Tory organizers, strategists, public relations types, bagmen and assorted hangers-on jumped onto the Campbell bandwagon. So many of these eager helpers were senior people that to keep them all feeling as important as they thought they were, Campbell's campaign managers dished out titles like cups of coffee. By April 8 the Campbell campaign had no fewer than forty-four titled senior positions and twelve other advisors. Jean Charest's campaign, by comparison, had twelve titled staffers and four strategists.

Along with Gilles Loiselle, head of the Treasury Board, came his son Frédéric, one of two deputy directors of operations. Loiselle senior was tagged with the heavy-handed recruitment of

Pierre Blais, the new Justice Minister, whom he allegedly told to get on side or lose his portfolio.[16]

Among the non-Quebec group were some of the country's most notorious political spin doctors and influence peddlers. There was Patrick Kinsella, the former advisor to Socred Premier Bill Bennett and a veteran Tory organizer in Ontario campaigns with the Big Blue Machine. Also on the list was David Angus, who was the head of the PC Canada Fund when the "Guccigate" scandal broke in 1987. (It was revealed that Mulroney had been given $308,000 to pay for expensive renovations to 24 Sussex Drive — an "orgy of opulence," according to opposition critics.[17])

Others from the Ontario wing of the party with long experience and considerable influence were former Ontario Conservative leader Larry Grossman, Ontario party president and right-winger Thomas Long, and vice-president Glen Wright along with former Solicitor General Doug Lewis, Communications Minister Perrin Beatty, and two of Beatty's organizers, Michael Coates and Bruce McLellan, a senior executive of the public relations firm Hill and Knowlton.

Senator Norm Atkins was particularly enthusiastic. Atkins, described by Mulroney biographer Clare Hoy as "the ruthless chief mechanic of Ontario's legendary Big Blue Machine,"[18] reportedly went around early on in the campaign telling other candidates, including Barbara McDougall, that they would be humiliated and that they should withdraw.[19] And then there was Paul Curley. Curley is the former Tory party national director who currently owns Advance Planning and Communications, the firm hired by National Defence to sell the EH101 helicopters to the public and to the cabinet. He managed convention week for Campbell.

British Columbia was well represented as well. Besides Kinsella, there was David Camp, the son of Dalton Camp, who was appointed to run Campbell's campaign even before Mulroney announced that he was stepping down. In addition, there was Gerry Lampert, a noted heavyweight and former assistant to both Bill Vander Zalm and Joe Clark.

The Quebec backroom boys provided Campbell with what she needed in that province: a network of hardball players with connections going deep into the constituency organizations across the province. They provided her with the immediate advantage of getting a leg up on the delegate selection process. That, after all, is what counts in the end. The public image of the candidates was less important in winning the leadership than it would be in winning the next election. In the federal election, the backroom players would have less involvement in policy than in the key area of attempting to rebuild the old coalition of right-wing nationalists.

As it turned out, all the high-powered and high-priced help backfired. The schmoozing, in combination with an uncritical media, made the public angry. By the end of March, just a week after Campbell declared her candidacy, media outlets were getting heavy flak from their readers and viewers over the easy ride that she was getting. *The Globe and Mail* printed six letters on March 31 displaying varying degrees of doubt and anger at Campbell's attitudes and the media's lacklustre job. Suddenly, the media seemed to wake up and take more notice of what Campbell was saying — and not saying. Her lack of substance quickly became the backdrop for articles covering her appearances. Yet Campbell continued to use the same phrases to convey the same message about "inclusiveness" to an increasingly sceptical audience of reporters and voters. Pollster Angus Reid was surprised: "This inclusiveness ploy has a shelf life of about ten days."[20] Suddenly the leadership was Campbell's to lose.

Initially the Tories thought themselves fortunate that Jean Charest, the baby-faced right-wing federalist from Quebec, had decided to enter the race at all. Until he reversed his decision to stay out, the field looked embarrassingly thin. A handful of also-rans were up against the obvious winner — Kim Campbell. When Charest finally announced his candidacy, it did not long remain a secret that Mulroney had contacted his Quebec lieutenants, directing them to ensure that enough money went Charest's way to make the race a good one. What Mulroney had not counted on was that Campbell's lacklustre performance was a far greater boost for Charest than leftover cash from Mulroney's bagmen.

Campbell should have done better than she did. She was smart, quick-witted and articulate, and many of her earlier adversaries in Vancouver testified to her ability to debate and handle tough situations. But this race was different. In previous political battles, she relied primarily on her own abilities and her own judgement. She ran the show and picked good staff to assist her. Here, Campbell was running for the national leadership of a party that she had belonged to for only five years. This affected the amount of control that she could exercise over the campaign. That did not simply mean the enormous problem of logistics. No candidate could or would want to be involved in the day-to-day grind. But Campbell did not seem to have control of any aspect of the campaign. She was a politician who had very few close political friends and virtually no political networks outside her Vancouver riding. To consider running for the leadership, she had to place herself in the hands of existing political networks and trust political operatives she probably had never met.

That would have been manageable if it had been the relatively coherent network provided by Mulroney, which included not only his Quebec crew but a good contingent from the Big Blue Machine in Ontario. But the Campbell bandwagon had the effect of bringing into the campaign dozens of organizers, public relations experts, lobbyists and fund raisers. Suddenly there were two huge tasks: actually running for the leadership — travelling, making speeches, creating her image as a leader — and also imposing some kind of order on the huge support group she found flocking to her camp. She would have to decide whom to trust on the bandwagon. With only a few months of preparation, it was no easy task.

Losing Support

By April, there was almost daily criticism that Campbell had no substance and that her message of inclusiveness sounded shallow. Yet Campbell and her managers seemed incapable of adapting. Charest was picking up support among Tories but, equally important, he was impressing journalists and voters. Campbell's so-called winability factor was showing the first signs of tarnish. It was her apparent winability that had caused the campaign to go her way. She would live or die by it in a Tory party that cared about little else.

Signs that Campbell was less impressive than people had been led to believe had come early. At a speech in Kitchener, Campbell continued her rhetorical flourishes: "My vision of Canada is of a Canadian renaissance." A reporter in the crowd later claimed that even her fans were left wondering about policies.[21] She bewildered her audience with her vision of Canada: "An openness to creativity and to the voices and ideas of those who have previously been silent. A modern economy. The restoration of sound values in public service. The rebirth of hope that government can be a force for good rather a source of division. In short, an era of hope, reform and renewal."[22] If Campbell knew what all this meant, she may have been the only one of the 450 in the room who did.

It was the classic frontrunner campaign. Said one Campbell organizer: "If you're still building momentum with this soft media stuff — her personality, her style, her being in touch — without saying a damn thing about policy, you stick to it."[23] The same day that her organizer made this statement, however, another member of her team was worrying out loud about the possibility that Tory heavyweight Hugh Segal might enter the race.[24] Ontario organizers and MPs were having second thoughts about Campbell, in part because she was seen to be faltering and in part because the right wing did not trust her on economic matters, where her cabinet posts had given her little experience.

It would be fair to suggest that there were strong elements of sexism and revenge in the move to draft Segal, the quintessential backroom boy and Mulroney's chief of staff. The effort was being spearheaded by four cabinet ministers — all but one of whom had considered running themselves. Michael Wilson, the most embittered loser, was joined by Bernard Valcourt, Bill McKnight of Saskatchewan and Otto Jelinek.

Segal took several days to decide, and he put a real scare into the Campbell campaign. Many wondered aloud why Segal, a long-time Red Tory, would be willingly recruited by the most right-wing members of the cabinet. His answer cleared things up. He said that the old distinctions no longer held. "We're all Mulroney Tories now."[25] To the relief of Campbell's backers, Segal's threat evaporated.

But the reasons for it did not. Under pressure from the other leadership hopefuls, the party decided to organize five separate two-hour debates among the candidates, some to take place before the delegates were chosen, some after. It should have been Campbell's place to shine. But Campbell, the quick study in her Justice portfolio and strong debater in her own milieu, was now a creature of her spin doctors. The first debate took place in April. Prepping up until the last minute — she was the only candidate who declined the walk-through of the set and as a result had problems with her mike and chair height — she was the voice of her countless advisors. And she failed to impress.

Campbell's performance was universally judged to be flat and subdued, in contrast with her image of being feisty and on the offensive. Off-camera, she "appeared to be either pouting or frowning most of the time."[26] Once again she declined to talk policies but focused on "process." One of her advisors later explained that Mulroney's government had lots of good policies and they had kept him at 20 percent in the polls for three years: it would not be good policies that reversed Tory fortunes.[27]

It had been considered important for Campbell to do well in the first debate and the *Globe* headline, "Campbell advisors say forum not a disaster," was the last thing Campbell's backers wanted to read. The first debate was so important because of the expectation that she would not fare well in the second, which was to be held in Quebec. It was conceded that Charest would have the home-field advantage in his own province. Now he would be going into a sure victory with one win already under his belt.

The Montreal debate took place on April 21. In the midst of a spirited discussion of minority rights, Charest took the high road, as he had in the first debate. Describing Canada as a culture of diversity, Charest argued that it was the duty of the prime minister to enhance biculturalism. He pledged leadership on the language issue, saying that he would do for the English-speaking minority in Quebec what Mulroney had done for francophones in Manitoba.

Campbell took the low road, repeating her stance established in the first debate where she had stated that it was "not a prime minister's business" to interfere in Quebec's language law. But this time her efforts to extricate herself from any responsibility for minority rights went to bizarre lengths. In the heat of a debate on language, she declared Quebec's civil code legal system to be the issue and an advantage for Canada. "As former Minister of Justice I can say that we can touch all systems of law [as a result of the code], especially in the new democracies of Eastern and Central Europe. This gives us an incredible political and economic advantage. I would do nothing to reduce this economic promise for us."[28]

This comment was so completely out of place in the context of the discussion that no one responded to it. It was a surprisingly crude attempt to avoid the issue of language in front of a Quebec audience. But more than that, it revealed a candidate who could not adapt to the challenge of the moment. Charest had thrown her a curve and, in response, she read her reply from prepared notes clearly meant for some other context.

But if there was any doubt about her intention to leave the language issue strictly to the government of Quebec, she cleared it away with the last sentence of her closing remarks: "I say to you tonight ... that Kim Campbell will never allow any bureaucrat or any interest groups to revive the arrogant, domineering, centralizing federalism of the Trudeau-Chrétien years which led Canada to its ruin."[29] The significance of this statement and its shrillness was not lost on Ottawa-watchers. Commentators immediately tagged Campbell with speaking the words of her chief Quebec organizer, the strong nationalist Marcel Masse. Hugh Winsor observed: "The targeting of the bureaucracy provided the first clue to the line's authorship. Mr. Masse acquired a reputation for inflicting rants about bureaucrats on his fellow ministers when he was in the cabinet. Ms. Campbell, on the other hand, has developed good working relationships with bureaucrats. And she has never devoted a millisecond to a condemnation of the centralizing agenda of the Trudeau-Chrétien years."[30] Others noted that the phrase "centralizing and domineering federalism" was also used by Robert Bourassa, an integral member of the alliances Mulroney had built in Quebec.

The Quebec forum revealed for the first time just how deliberately Campbell was following in Mulroney's footsteps in her strategy for winning the next election. To revive the old coalition that Mulroney had brought together to win the 1984 election, she had to appeal to Quebec nationalism.

The implication of opportunism was impossible to miss. For a candidate with no network of her own and a very short record in the party and government, Campbell simply had little choice. If she wanted to win, she had to give her campaign over to the power brokers who had the capacity to win a campaign for her. What price she might have to pay later on was a question she would answer when the time came.

The impression that Campbell was the mouthpiece for Quebec Tory nationalists was reinforced by her delivery as well. While virtually all the other candidates attempted, at least, to speak spontaneously, Campbell was apparently so unaccustomed to the message she was delivering that she had to read it, which she did for half the evening.

In a post-debate discussion, Quebec reporters noted Campbell's difficulty with the content and the language. "Everyone's been saying that she's perfectly bilingual, but she's not. It's the way she explains herself," said Marie-Claude Lortie of *La Presse*. "It's the flow, the confidence, it's just not there. Sheila Copps shows that it's not important to have every word just so, it's important to just go for it. It's probably going to disappoint a lot of people who were expecting more of her French."[31]

Sarah Scott of the *Gazette* was surprised at how much better the other candidates were than Campbell. "[They] didn't refer to their notes quite as much as Campbell did. She spent a lot of time reading the notes, obviously nervous about the language ... I thought she was still quite devoid of content."[32]

It bears repeating that the other major plank in Campbell's strategy for taking Quebec involved patronage and helicopters. Joe Clark learned the hard way that Conservatives expect to be rewarded just as Liberals do. When Clark failed to deliver the plums to hard-working Tory operatives after he won the leadership in 1976, many turned against him. The test Campbell had to pass to prove she understood the game was the helicopter test. Come hell or high water the EH101 helicopter deal had to go through.

With both Marcel Masse and Paul Curley prominent in her campaign, it was not likely that Campbell would be allowed to forget just how critical the helicopters were to her leadership bid and, more important, to her taking Quebec in the next federal election. Two billion dollars worth of contracts to Montreal-based Paramax bought a huge amount of political goodwill in the right places. And while Campbell must have dearly wished to get the helicopters off her back, she had made a deal that had to be kept, whatever the price to her campaign and her election prospects.

On May 5, supported by a phalanx of generals, Defence Department bureaucrats and her personal entourage of advisors, she made clear one more time that the helicopter order was written in stone. She announced defence cuts — abandoned missile projects, delayed improvements to fighter jets and most importantly the laying off of 5,000 more soldiers and defence staff — then said: "There is, however, one project that is essential to the modernization program that will not be deferred."[33] The $5.6 billion worth of EH101 helicopters.

The day after the Montreal debate, the Campbell campaign was widely seen to be in serious disarray. Many questions were being asked about why a candidate with such apparent skills seemed unable to capitalize on what had been an enormous lead. The crisis was apparently recognized even within the campaign, for the day after the poor performance in Montreal, there was a major reorganization of the Campbell team. Patrick Kinsella was brought in to help give the campaign some coherence. There was no shortage of "hardball players" on the team, so the decision to promote Kinsella to the centre of the campaign may have been Campbell's personal choice. Kinsella, who had first persuaded Campbell to run in 1983 for the Socreds, was one of the few political associates Campbell had known for more than a few years. Lowell Murray, the Tory senator who led the fight to get the GST passed in the Senate, was also brought on board.

Kim Campbell's Policies

It is not surprising that the policy centrepiece of Campbell's run at the Tory leadership dealt with the debt. She has a long record of enthusiastic support for restraint programs. The deliberately created debt hysteria provided her and the other Tory candidates with the ideal target in their policy pronouncements. Each tried to outdo the other in predicting how soon they could balance the budget.

Campbell claimed that she could balance the budget in five years — only to be outbid by Charest, who came up with four. But neither candidate offered a specific strategy for accomplishing this huge task. When Campbell announced her "five-year plan," she gave the same response that she had used for weeks: "Canadians don't want 30-second sound bite answers."[34] It was especially clear that Campbell had no specific plan when Reform Party leader Preston Manning put forward his plan, which was very detailed. Later into the campaign, Campbell retreated to her inclusiveness theme, saying that she wanted to consult Canadians about where to cut. The vague themes she was willing to outline later — restructuring government, cutting cabinet size, limiting MPs' pensions and reducing the public sector — amounted to little more than financial tinkering if she was serious about cutting $35 billion from federal spending.[35]

She hedged on the issue of new taxes. She said on several occasions that spending cuts were the way to go. "I think reducing the size of government and government spending is really the only answer. New taxes aren't the answer."[36] She declined, however, to pledge herself, Bush-style, to no new taxes.

In an unusual departure from her policy vagueness, Campbell took a position on the Bank of Canada that could have been written by its current head, John Crow. The Bank, already independent of government direction, would have an even freer hand under Campbell. She stated in connection with her deficit reduction plan that she favoured "strengthening the independence of the bank of Canada ... expressly placing price stability at the forefront of its mandate."[37] In short, the Bank would remain the single-minded inflation-fighting institution it has been under the entire Mulroney régime. Making that role an explicit part of its mandate would lock future governments into a policy obsession of the current Mulroney government. Many economists have raised serious doubts about the Bank's high-interest, inflation-fighting policies in a time of recession.

All the candidates seemed to bury the notion of "sacred trusts" once and for all. Mulroney's famous line about the inviolability of Canada's welfare state and his subsequent violation of his pledge would not be repeated by any Tory this time around. This time, there would be no pledge to violate. In fact, as the campaign unfolded, Campbell became gradually more aggressive on the issue, at first hinting that universality had to be re-examined and then explicitly referring to the principle as "ridiculous." Asked at the end of April about the fate of universality and whether Canadians would tolerate ending it, Campbell replied: "I think Canadians are much in advance of government, and, if I may say, the media on a lot of these issues. I think Canadians understand the situation we're in ... .We can't afford the principle for all our programs now, and I think we have to deal with it."[38]

Campbell then took the issue one step further, entering waters that even the evangelical free enterpriser Preston Manning had backed away from. Asked whether she would consider the imposition of user fees for medicare, she replied: "If it was the consensus of working with the provinces on how to rejig our social programs, then yes."[39] Everything was on the table, said Campbell. She spoke vaguely enough, however, to allow herself some room to claim that she had been misquoted as supporting user fees — a tack she took days later, after Brian Mulroney stated that he thought user fees were a mistake.

Medicare user fees are a direct assault on universality because they deny those with low incomes equal access to medical services. Campbell, having already abandoned the principle of universality, was scarcely credible quibbling over details like user fees. The Mulroney government has already set the stage for the end to universality through its legislation removing Ottawa from the health funding formula by the year 2007. That alone will end universality, because it will cut the provinces loose from the Canada Health Act and permit any and all government mechanisms to cheapen the system. Campbell has in effect signalled that she would end universality more directly and therefore more quickly.

All these policy initiatives seem to have been quickly cobbled together in response to critical comments from the media. Campbell's retreat on user fees and her embarrassing lack of detail on deficit reduction suggested that her team could not get out of the frontrunner mode even after the battle for the leadership had narrowed considerably.

There were no apparent policy advisors behind these platform tidbits and certainly no coherent economic plan for a country mired in recession and high unemployment. Indeed, in contrast to some of her opponents, Campbell seemed unaware that there were any problems with the economy. Nowhere did she address the issue in the first month and a half of the campaign; she never referred to unemployment or to the recession and certainly not to the problem of poverty. This contrasts with Charest, who matched Campbell on deficit reduction and attacks on universality, but referred several times to the need to deal with unemployment and poverty.

Campbell's statements about what she would not do were often as revealing as the policies she promoted. Child care, for example, the issue she had so much trouble with in early interviews following her announcement, was simply not on. To applause from her Tory audience, Campbell declared that her government's earlier pledge to finance a national child care program was "beyond our economic means." But yet again, she hedged: "It is an issue that I want to look at more closely. I am concerned about it but the kind of things we looked at in 1988 are just not economically feasible."[40]

To help those reporters or members of the public who were trying to get to the bottom of "inclusiveness," a 1-800 number was set up. It was supposed to allow people to engage in the process, but it turned out to be a pitch for prospective Tory party members. The message, from Campbell herself: "Hi, this is Kim Campbell.

Thanks very much for calling my help line. You know over the coming months we have a chance to forge a new vision for our party, our government and our country, but it's going to take a lot of hard work and there's lots we have to do. My vision of Canada is an inclusive one where we reach out to all Canadians and invite them to participate in building our new futures ... I hope you'll stay on the line to find out how you can help me." Next, a male voice came on the line: "If you would like to make a donation, press 1; to join the Conservative Party of Canada, press 2; to become a Kim Campbell volunteer, press 3." The caller could also press 4 to express his or her opinion on any topic, but by the time most people got that far they might reasonably conclude that if they had not pressed 1, 2 or 3 they might not be included after all.

It appears that inclusiveness for Campbell is reduced to joining a political party — preferably, her political party. And her political reforms, announced April 19 at a campaign rally, emphasized this as well. Of three specific proposals, one was to require "her own party to consult its members on policy more than once every four years."[41]

Campbell also established as policy a measure that was specifically designed to restrict the influence of advocacy groups, a form of "inclusion" that had been born out of social movements in the sixties and promoted by the Trudeau government. Campbell had earlier proposed "to make the budget process more open by requiring interest groups to disclose publicly the special favours they are seeking."[42] In her policy session with delegates at the convention, she went even further, saying that she did not believe advocacy groups should be funded at all. Afterwards, she backed off that position, but her sentiments were clear.

There can be little doubt about what Campbell meant by interest groups in this context. She is a right-wing conservative, and conservatives, led by their Republican counterparts in the United States, have for years used the term "interest group" pejoratively to undermine groups representing women, the poor, aboriginal people, labour, gays and lesbians, and others who are attempting to make their voices heard. Her repeated claims to have welcomed input from such groups when she was Justice Minister have been vigorously denied by groups in her own constituency and by national organizations.

On occasion this tension between her partisan view of "inclusiveness" and that of advocacy groups is stated explicitly: "We should be reaching out to all Canadians and saying 'Come and work with us, be part of us.' If we ask, they will come, they are coming *now*. We are inviting Canadians to assume the responsibility of citizenship ... We can show the world it's possible to transcend special interests and petty differences."[43] This statement only makes sense if it is assumed that Campbell means people of varied interests are joining the Conservative Party — transcending the tendency to join "interest groups."

Campbell's other proposals for democratic reform were mostly commitments to examine certain possibilities. Two that she committed herself to were more freedom for MPs speaking up in the House of Commons and tighter control on lobbyists. The first, clearly a necessary reform, is now promised by virtually everyone except Brian Mulroney. And it would be difficult for Campbell to reconcile this promise to loosen party discipline with a speech she made at Harvard University in November 1992, extolling the virtues of party discipline: "Party discipline, in my view, is one of the major bulwarks against the power of private interests. It is one of the major intergrating factors in government. It enables a parliamentary system to function." [44]

As for control on lobbyists, it is fair to ask how the dozens of lobbyists on her campaign team would feel about it. Tories, lobbyists in particular, expect rewards for the work they do on leadership campaigns. Their livelihood depends on it. Restrictions on their activities would not be viewed favourably and Campbell, more than any of her opponents in the race, would be extremely vulnerable to pressure from those who were key to her leadership victory.

Even when announcing reforms regarding her "inclusive politics" theme, Campbell could not avoid manipulating the audience. Behind her as she spoke was a double row of carefully selected supporters — representing all ages, both sexes and people of colour. Although Campbell was probably not directly responsible for this crude display of ersatz "inclusiveness," she bears ultimate responsibility for it.

As for the remainder of Campbell's reforms, they were, like many of her policy pronouncements, commitments to "consider" or to "further study," or they were introduced with escape clauses such as "we should consider whether ... " or "on the one hand ... on the other hand." These were commitments that would be easily jettisoned whenever the need arose.

When Campbell presented the package as "my views and my suggestions," the Liberals and New Democrats were quick to point out that they had both presented parliamentary reform packages virtually identical to those Campbell was pledging to "study." The government had rejected them.

Campbell also released a broad policy document called "Canada at the Millennium." It outlined the completion of the Mulroney agenda in policies that covered everything from taxation to education to social programs. It received little media attention. The document called for the elimination of most regulation of corporations in order to save money, more tax breaks for corporations and investors to encourage growth, criteria for privatization that would see the selling off of most crown corporations, a continued dedication to the fight against inflation, the opening up of our manufacturing base to even more "free trade" agreements and the elimination of universality. But it did not really matter if these policies were well known or not. Campbell's campaign for the Tory leadership would be won where it had always been won: on the ground.

The Leadership Convention

While policies and debating points may have a real impact on the broader Canadian public, they are only one factor in a leadership race. In this leadership race they were secondary. Because the organization on the ground was the first key to victory, the candidate with the best organization could weather the storms stirred up by a poor performance or vague policies. That was the case with Kim Campbell. By the weekend of May 8–9, Campbell had nearly 45 percent of the constituency delegates sewn up, twice as many as Charest. The also-rans were not even in the counting. Campbell's biggest worry was the number of undecided — over 30 percent in mid-May — but even here she was confident. She would need only one in six of the undecided to push her over the top on a first ballot.[1]

Campbell's opponents were clearly right in pushing for early debates. When Campbell gave a lacklustre performance in the first two debates, Charest suddenly became a credible candidate. Although Campbell did much better in the third debate — loosening the strings of her handlers — the doubts had been sown. The media, stung by their fawning attention to Campbell, suddenly "discovered" Charest and promoted him as a natural debater and born leader. Polls in late April showed that Charest would fare as well as Campbell in a federal election,[2] a result that did not affect the election of slates at the constituency level but did pose a potential threat to Campbell among the undecided delegates.

From the outset, Campbell had built her bandwagon on the perception that she could win the next federal election. Having promoted that aspect of her candidacy, losing the mantle of Tory saviour meant that even by her own standards, she was no longer the natural leader. As a woman candidate, that was particularly risky. Campbell was, after all, in the party least accepting of women. Like the British Conservative Party, the Canadian Tory party would consider a woman for leader only if she could virtually guarantee the best showing in the contest for power. If Campbell's so-called winability factor were seen to slip seriously, the sexism that permeated the Tory party could suddenly be given free rein.

In a more normal leadership convention, the polls showing Charest gaining on Campbell among voters at large might have played a less important role. When Mulroney and Clark were battling it out, the fight was between two longtime Tory activists who had spent the better part of their adult lives labouring for the Conservative cause. They had loyal friends and debts owing, which meant that those who initially committed themselves were very likely to stay on board. Stories in the daily press had little impact — and in any case there was scarcely anything worth knowing about the main contenders that was not already known, at least within the party.

None of this held true for Campbell or Charest. The loyalty factor was much weaker and the potential for "committed" delegates to drift away was considerable for both candidates. This factor was especially potent in a party that had begun to see itself as the government party. After decades as the alternative to the Liberals, the Tories had been in power for nine years and had become accustomed to running the show. Winning was everything. The broader public's perception of the candidates took on added importance. A gaffe here, a misstatement there, could count for a lot among a potentially fickle body of delegates.

The Campbell Persona: Gaffes or Candour?

Over a period of eight days in May, Campbell seemed to produce a political lifetime's worth of gaffes and misstatements. One barely died down before another took its place. For the frontrunner, watching her lead erode under the fierce scrutiny of the media must have been a lot like a nasty roller-coaster ride.

The first serious blunder came on May 13, at the end of an otherwise competent, if unexciting, performance in the Vancouver leadership forum. Concluding her comments with a reference to her priority, dealing with the deficit, Campbell described those who disagreed with her and the Tories on the importance of the deficit as the "enemies of Canadians."[3] The misstep wiped out any advantage she might have managed with the rest of her performance.

She pointed out after the forum that she had attempted to soften the impact with the words, "I use that term mildly."[4] But the damage had been done. It reminded the public of the use by Mulroney of the phrase "enemies of Canada" to describe those who opposed the Charlottetown accord — one of the factors in the deal's defeat.

The "enemies of Canadians" comment would probably have faded into the background if not for the next revelation. This time published comments she had made in January 1993 during a candid, three-hour conversation with Peter C. Newman did the damage. Parts of the interview were published in *Vancouver* Magazine, a small-circulation monthly. The piece had been around for over a week and ignored by the media. Ironically, Campbell's campaign organizers thought it so flattering that they copied it and mailed it to reporters.

The article was, for the most part, a very uncritical profile of Campbell, showing an engaging, open side at a time when many people had forgotten that part of her personality. It was meant to present her candour as a plus. But once again Campbell's own words reinforced the perception that she was a "loose cannon." A seemingly angry shot at politically apathetic Canadians once again seemed to reveal her arrogance and tendency to belligerence. "I don't believe that democratic institutions run on auto-pilot. The thing that infuriates me is apathy. People who boast about how they've never been involved in a political party. Who do they think is working to keep this society intact so that they can have the luxury of sitting back and being such condescending SOBs? To hell with them."[5]

Campbell would later defend this and other quotations in the article as examples her "candour." Perhaps. But others saw it as offensive and an example of poor judgement. What the comment revealed was just how unaware Campbell really was of the political cynicism she and her fellow Tories had created in the past five years. A large part of that cynicism was due to her government's contempt for people who *did* get directly involved in the politics of the country — or tried to.

It is fair to say that at few points in Canadian history were more Canadians involved in the politics of their country than during the Tories' efforts to impose the GST. Hundreds of thousands of Canadians signed petitions, joined organizations, demonstrated in the streets, phoned or wrote their MPs — demanding that the GST be withdrawn. But for Campbell this was "interest group" activity and simply irrelevant. It was not participation, by her definition, which requires joining a political party.

While Campbell was rightly taken to task for that comment, she clearly got a bum rap on her remark about Catholicism: "I got confirmed as an Anglican the year I was here [at a Catholic boarding school], I suppose as a way of warding off the demons of the papacy, or whatever."[6]

While the comment raised questions about her political judgement in a country where 46 percent of the population identify themselves as Catholic, it had nothing to do with religious bigotry. The offending line was delivered in the context of describing her year at a Catholic boarding school. Reading the rest of her comments strongly suggests that Campbell has no animosity towards the Catholic Church. For her part, Campbell said she respected "spiritual principles" but had always been suspicious of organized religions "because of the way they treated women."[7]

A third item in the Newman piece gave more evidence of Campbell's tendency to treat others in a rather snide and nasty way. Referring to Joe Clark, her cabinet colleague and, now at least, a figure widely respected among Tories, she said, "I wouldn't want to win the leadership on a kind of technical basis, the way Joe Clark did ... He was the least hated candidate."[8] Besides being an inaccurate assessment of history, it was again seen as bad judgement.

Campbell was defended by much of the media on the papal demons comment, particularly over the rough ride she was given in the *Toronto Star*. But the hiatus did not last long. Along with Charest, Campbell had earlier on admitted to having smoked marijuana at university. She was faced with a reference to her admission in a media scrum. Was it not hypocritical to be sending people to jail for smoking marijuana when she had committed the same criminal act with impunity? asked a reporter. "I'm not sure," said Campbell, "that what I did brought me in breach of the criminal law as a matter of fact. It's not a crime to smoke marijuana."[9] Pressed on this remarkable claim, Campbell did not back off.

The result was as immediate as it was predictable. Reporters ran off to interview expert people with an interest in the issue. An RCMP official simply contradicted her and stated the obvious: possession is illegal and you have to possess the drug in order to smoke it. The most lasting image was that of lawyer Clayton Ruby who burst into theatrical guffaws on hearing her comments.

Campbell and Charest had been given high marks earlier in the campaign for admitting that they had smoked marijuana *and* inhaled it. Their candour was contrasted to Bill Clinton's dubious claim to have smoked pot but *without* inhaling. Campbell could have left it at that. But her comment that *smoking* marijuana is not illegal seemed to suggest once again that she always had to be right. It was a comment more worthy of a teenager arguing with her mother than a would-be prime minister.

Campbell went on to make a flippant comparison of a marijuana conviction to a speeding ticket. But, as the reporter pointed out, a speeding infraction does not get you banned from travelling to the United States. Most of the criminal convictions for illicit drugs in Canada are for simple possession of marijuana. Was Campbell insensitive to the problems faced by thousands of otherwise law-abiding Canadians who received criminal records for this minor offence? If she really thought that it was this insignificant, would she support taking it out of the criminal code or reducing sentences? She told reporters that she thought the sentences appropriate and saw no reason for decriminalizing the use of marijuana. Indeed, her former Justice Department just days later announced that it was increasing the severity of the sentences in addition to making it an offence to even ask for an illicit drug.[10]

Throughout her political career, Campbell has demonstrated an inability to admit that she is wrong or that she has any faults. Yet she felt obliged to call news conferences to defend herself from media attacks and from her opponents who were beginning to sense that they *could* criticize her without being accused of overstepping the line. Campbell was being characterized as "reckless," "callous and élitist" and as having poor judgement. But she would not admit that she had said anything wrong or made any mistakes. In her defence she insisted, "Everything I have said was sensible."[11] She told *The Toronto Star* that she found it "amusing that people are making a lot out of half-quotations."[12] Campbell blamed the media and insisted that the issue was simply that she "had a different way of expressing myself ... But I'm not prepared to change."[13] Calling the media's response "knee-jerk," she asked, "Are you going to play the old games, the 'getcha, gotcha' game where you grab a word out of something and make something out of it that it was clearly not ... or are you going to allow a politician to be a person?"[14]

Unfortunately for Campbell, the answer was quite obviously "No." Worse, a lot of Canadians gave the same answer. Polls began to show Charest gaining on Campbell as a result of the gaffes and acerbic comments. But Campbell could not — or would not — change. She had told Newman in the interview that she was not sure she could be prime minister on her own terms but that she did not want to accept the job any other way. As Hugh Winsor remarked, "It says volumes about Ms. Campbell that she is so determined to prove she was right in the case of Mr. Newman's article ... that she is prepared to explain the circumstances of every phrase."[15] The Newman interview itself revealed the same inability to accept that she had any faults. Asked by Newman about her shortcomings, Campbell replied: "I mean ... let's see, what are my shortcomings? Now that will sound really arrogant if I can't think of any. I know: I don't like using the telephone."[16]

Trial by Polls

From the middle of May, numerous polls showed that Campbell's "winability" factor was slipping. These were mostly polls of voters and not of delegates. Campbell's organization remained extremely strong on the ground, where, according to conventional wisdom, it was supposed to count.

For Campbell, the polls became a reminder of the volatility of the Canadian populace and the unpredictability of the media. They also underlined just how far the country and its political culture had to go before a woman prime minister would be considered normal. Through most of the campaign, the media were generally not overtly sexist in their coverage. There was no commentary about what the woman candidate wore, which in years past was considered standard, and there was little more than passing reference to Campbell's two divorces. But the rapidity with which the media turned on Campbell, and the extent of the coverage of her every move even after Charest had closed the gap, suggested that Campbell was being treated differently than she would have been had she been a man.

Yet most of the coverage, including earlier commentary on her lack of policy specifics, was legitimate. Judgement was an issue; personality was an issue; her ability to listen to the views of others was an issue. The fact that her political performance was mediocre may have given freer rein to the sexism latent in the electorate, the media and the Tory party. Unfortunately for Campbell, her tendency to arrogance and her frequent gaffes lent some credence to criticisms which would otherwise have sounded sexist.

The importance of the winability factor in swaying delegates seemed to be confirmed in a COMPAS poll conducted for *The Financial Post* magazine and the *Sun* newspapers between May 28 and 30 and released on June 2, just eleven days before the convention vote. It suggested that 91 percent of the delegates "acknowledged following the opinion polls and 60 percent said poll results play a part in their decisions about which candidate to support."[17]

The poll was not good news for Campbell. It showed that going into the convention Campbell had 46 percent of the delegates, virtually the same percentage she had enjoyed a month earlier. Charest was now up to 41 percent. Taking delegates' second-ballot preferences into account and assuming movement of Campbell and Charest delegates, the poll showed a second-ballot victory for Charest by a margin of 56 percent to 44 percent. With no movement of the frontrunners' delegates and adding in second ballot preferences, Campbell was predicted to win by a 51 to 49 percent margin.

The details of the poll demonstrated the impact of Campbell's controversial comments. Fully 68 percent of delegates polled characterized Campbell as "unstable or unpredictable" and saw her as the "most unfriendly" candidate. Another test was how "uncomfortable" delegates would be in voting for various candidates: 32 percent said they would be "uncomfortable" voting for Campbell, while only 7 percent said that of Charest. The poll also revealed that Campbell's early lead as the candidate best able to win in Quebec had been devastated. Seventy-seven percent of delegates polled said Charest would be best able to beat the Bloc Québécois, as compared to 21 percent for Campbell. In ability to beat the Liberals' Jean Chrétien, Campbell was still holding her own: 42 percent compared to 54 percent for Charest.

The COMPAS poll also asked delegates about the two leading candidates' "chief weaknesses." The biggest deficit for Campbell was her "arrogant/unstable personality" (45 percent) followed by "does not know how to handle the media" (7 percent). Charest had two deficiencies: "too young" (30 percent) and "he is a Quebecer"(17 percent). But the poll also suggested that Charest's Quebec origins were not as great a deficit as might have been expected. Seventy percent of delegates polled said that it did not matter where the next leader came from; 65 percent said that age did not matter, either.

Other than Charest, according to the poll, the only candidate to gain in delegates over the course of the campaign had been Alberta's Jim Edwards, who had gone from 1 percent of the delegates in March to 9 percent. The poll also predicted that 73 percent of Edwards's supporters would go to Charest.

While Campbell was fighting off the effects of her own mistakes, Charest seemed to have developed a "teflon man" character. Despite several stories in late May about potential scandals and political indiscretions and although his record in cabinet was dismal, Charest got an easy ride. This continued even after it seemed that the media scrutiny of Campbell had given him an edge. Although Campbell enjoyed good press in the beginning, once she was solidly in first place the media examined every detail of what she said. Charest was never put under scrutiny in the same way that Campbell was.

Although the polls clearly showed that Campbell's *public* support had eroded, the headlines obscured one important fact: none of the polls indicated any significant erosion of Campbell's *delegate support.* The major papers were creating the impression of an irresistible momentum building for Charest. In the week leading up to the convention, the headlines about her growing unpopularity among Canadians screamed out at the readers. And three major papers, including *The Globe and Mail,* ran editorials supporting Charest for leader of the Conservatives.

But as it turned out, it was all irrelevant. As Charest said at the convention, "I just wish *The Globe and Mail* could vote." [18] The confusion about the momentum for Charest, the sagging popularity of Campbell, and Campbell's ultimate triumph could be found in the fact that they were running different races. Campbell, whose enormous lead in delegates was established almost before Charest was out of the starting gate, was pitching her campaign at the Tory delegates. Charest's only chance was to erode Campbell's committed delegates and so his campaign was pitched at Canadian voters in the hope that Campbell's problems would win him some of her delegates.

Gilles Loiselle, one of the first of the Quebec cabinet ministers to declare for Campbell, made that clear after Campbell won. He said the Campbell team decided to follow a certain strategy from the beginning that was different from the one Charest's camp followed. Charest directed his campaign towards the larger Canadian public, but Campbell's team decided to focus on the delegates. If her team had campaigned like that for the leadership, they would have used up all their ammunition for the real election.[19] Campbell's team decided simply to ignore the polls altogether, according to Michael Wilson, one of the late cabinet additions to Campbell's campaign and the seconder of her nomination: "We weren't going to be swayed by the pollsters and the media."[20] Mulroney's old fixer, Jean-Yves Lortie commented, "Mulroney would never have been prime minister if we had listened to polls."[21]

Charest's campaign strategy at the barbecues and small delegates' meetings across the country was to run a surrogate federal election campaign through the convention delegates. Time and again, news clips showed Charest urging delegates to not talk to other Tory members, but to ask their neighbours and their colleagues at work whom they would vote for in the next election.

For Campbell's team, for men like Patrick Kinsella who believe they can "move you to the other side of the ledger" at will, it was first things first. They really believe that with the careful manipulation of polling and with enough public relations massaging they can win any contest. They didn't care about Campbell's gaffes or the erosion of her public support. They would worry about that on June 14, the day after the convention. But for the media, and all the Canadians who relied on the media for their impressions of what was happening, the conventional wisdom held as the convention opened in Ottawa on June 11.

According to that wisdom, Campbell would have to make the speech of her life in order to ensure victory, even on the second ballot. And so all the attention focused on the speeches. Again, Charest played to the next election and gave a fiery and passionate speech, closing off by asking delegates, "Please, turn me loose on the Bloc Québécois." He played bluntly to his winability, more than before. Campbell's speech was more subdued and less spontaneous. Had she been speaking to the media or the broader Canadian public, the assessment of it as flat and uninspiring would have been appropriate. But Campbell and her organizers had been saying all weekend that they were close to winning it on the first ballot. She was not trying to win over the whole convention; she was not even trying to grab another 15 percent of the delegates. She was trying to keep the 50 percent she and her advisors thought they already had.

The raft of delegate interviews after the speeches once again reinforced the notion that the convention was swinging inexorably towards Charest. A good majority of a dozen or more undecided delegates interviewed by CBC and CTV said that the speeches had done it for them: they were going to Charest. *The Globe'*s Jeffrey Simpson saw the Campbell team at work, however. "In the hall ... I saw the old pros from Toronto, from Vancouver, from Montreal who knew what to do to organize. After her speech ... the organization did a very good job to reassure the troops, to organize them and to ensure that they would vote for her."[22]

The real unknown at the convention was how many delegates the popular Jim Edwards would take on the first ballot. Campbell may have been playing to Edwards and his supporters in her speech. She emphasized the deficit, referring to it three times, saying at one point that it was immoral for one generation to drive up a debt that the next generation will have to pay. Hinting at how she intends to run her election campaign, she expressed concern for "those things that distinguish us as a nation — our social programs, our quality of life, our prosperity." In the name of saving our social programs, we would have to cut them to get rid of the deficit.

Campbell reinforced her support for the Mulroney agenda and implicitly served notice on any party that might tamper with what Mulroney had done. "Canadians know that the challenges of the 90s cannot be overcome by replaying the 80s; by trying to undo at untold cost, policies that are right for Canada. They know that it would be wrong to throw away all that has been gained by the hard sacrifices and difficult adjustments they have made in recent years."[23]

The results of the first ballot stunned everyone in the hall except Campbell and her supporters. Campbell won an impressive 48 percent — 1,369 votes. Charest got 39 percent — 1,164. With a spread of nearly 300 votes, Charest had not even come close. The contest was all but over. If there was any doubt, it was removed within a few short minutes when, to the surprise again of almost everybody but Campbell, Jim Edwards moved to the Campbell compound in the Ottawa Civic Centre. Ironically, it was the high number of votes for Edwards — 307 — that had denied Campbell the first-ballot victory, and the high number for Campbell that led Edwards to move so quickly to her side. He was going to back the winner.

Charest and his supporters were devastated. They had won their campaign but lost the leadership. Among the public, Charest had bested Campbell. In fact, he proved the case that winability really was important in a contest that involved two relative unknowns within the party. Had Campbell changed her strategy under the pressure of the polls and editorials and tried to respond to Charest's campaign, she probably would have lost. But she kept to the strategy that had been laid out for her to follow.

The old boys and their old-style politics had won. Kinsella, the man who believes so strongly that he can "move you to do something that you may not have agreed is the logical thing to do" was right after all. In the end, they proved that they could take a candidate who by most accounts had virtually self-destructed and lead her to victory in spite of herself. That the old-boys' backroom politics had in fact made Canadian history by electing the country's first woman prime minister was, for them, an incidental irony.

Winners and Losers

Bill McKnight was wrong. The federal cabinet minister and Charest backer from Saskatchewan had embarrassed his candidate with the comment that if the Conservative Party stayed on the Campbell train it was headed for Jonestown, the site of a tragic mass suicide carried out by drinking a poison-laced beverage. He was confident, he claimed, that Tories "wouldn't drink Kim's kool aid."[24] It was a crude and tasteless comment, but one that obviously had resonance for many Tories, including, it was rumoured, Brian Mulroney himself. If Campbell's team was not thinking about the imminent federal election, other important Tories clearly were. In the weeks before the convention, two almost-rans, Joe Clark and Hugh Segal, had joined the Charest camp, ending any mystery as to why they had considered running in the first place.

As the convention gave a standing ovation to Campbell as she stood on stage after her second ballot win by a margin of 53 percent to 47 percent, Joe Clark looked glum. He was not clapping. Brian Mulroney was similarly downcast and, for whatever reason, broke with long Tory tradition by not addressing the convention as the outgoing leader. Perhaps they were thinking about Quebec. Mulroney had managed what no other Tory had ever managed in this country. He had put together a coalition in Quebec with staying power that had won the Tories back-to-back majority governments, an accomplishment that had eluded the party since the days of John A. Macdonald. Now Mulroney had rolled the dice on Campbell, handing her the Quebec machine that was supposed to preserve the coalition and deliver the province. He compounded the mistake by gambling again and urging Charest to run to make it a real race. The race exposed Campbell to the rigours of Quebec politics and she came up short.

While the anglophone Tories from the backrooms played it all as if there was no problem, Monique Vézina, the junior Minister for External Relations, was more truthful. "What concerns me about the Campbell victory is the deadly effect it will have on the seats in Quebec. I am convinced ... that the election of Kim Campbell ... would make us lose seats in Quebec. I am trying to imagine what she would be like at the Francophone summit."[25] Vézina was not the only Quebecer to express this analysis of the Campbell win. Lysiane Gagnon of *La Presse* said that the Liberals had initially written off Quebec and were not really counting on it to win a majority. At the beginning of the campaign it was not clear how Campbell would do in Quebec compared to Charest. "But," said Gagnon, "at the end it was obvious to everyone except the people working for Campbell."[26]

Gagnon was part of a panel who had interviewed Campbell on Radio Canada's public affairs show, "Le Point," the night before the leadership convention began. Campbell definitely was put to the test in this interview. The hard-hitting questions, which would have been tough to answer in any language, revealed what as prime minister she could expect from the Quebec media. For example, Benoît Aubin of *Le Devoir* asked her if she saw no contradiction in the fact that since the beginning of the leadership campaign she had talked about the politics of inclusion, yet her support seemed to have steadily eroded.

The interview demonstrated dramatically that Campbell's language skills were not up to the challenge of dealing with a rough ride from the Quebec media. She had to admit she was not perfectly bilingual and spoke French like a Vancouverite. Twice she had to say she did not understand the questions asked, and she could not come up with the French for simple words like "housing." Some of the things she said must have sounded quite strange to the French-speaking audience. She told one panelist that she had not "listened" to her when she obviously meant to say that she had not "heard" her, and she mixed up the words *l'immeuble* and *les meubles*. She also used quite odd constructions, such as *soulever les fonds* to say "raise funds" and *livrer la marchandise* when she meant "deliver the goods" — attempts to translate English phrases directly into French.

Campbell brought this awkward situation on herself by claiming that she was fluent in French, an exaggeration that was bound to catch up with her. Quebec journalists expressed criticism of her French in relation to the expectations that had been created at least partly by Campbell herself.

The Radio Canada interview demonstrated that when Campbell had to perform in French without written notes, she got into the kind of trouble that would severely handicap her not only in dealing with the French media but as well in diplomatic circles such as the Francophone Summit. Unable to use the kind of nuance in French that she is so skilled at in English, Campbell exposed the kind of crude politics she intended to use in Quebec. Asked how she would persuade Bloc Québécois supporters to vote Conservative, Campbell questioned why Quebecers would choose people "who could not deliver the goods. I think Quebecers know well that their interests are well protected by their representatives in the centre of power."[27] Campbell had attached herself to the most nationalist elements in the Conservative Party in Quebec. Gagnon pointed out that even though she "had been following the ideological line of Gilles Loiselle and Marcel Masse," her support seemed to be eroding in Quebec. That "ideological line" was exemplified in the EH101 helicopter deal and Masse's military spending spree in Quebec. It was crude and simple — try to buy off nationalist Quebecers by delivering the goods.

If Monique Vézina was concerned about Campbell's weakness in Quebec, her nationalist strategy in that province would be a gift to Preston Manning, a fact not lost on the NDP's Dave Barrett: "If she attempts to play a nationalist game in Quebec it will help the Reform Party in the west."[28] If Brian Mulroney and Joe Clark looked glum after Campbell's victory, there was good reason. Campbell was poised to grasp the worst of both worlds: a nationalist Quebec strategy that could flop in Quebec and inflame the West.

Campbell's political alignments and apparent election strategy for Quebec were not her only problems. Within two days of Campbell's victory, the divisions her campaign had created in the party started to come out into the open. One rural Quebec MP, André Plourde, declared that he might not run again because he did not think that Campbell could win in Quebec. Declaring that he was a businessman, he told reporters that he knew when he had a product he couldn't sell.[29] She was also attacked by businessman Conrad Black for her ties to "notorious Quebec nationalist" Marcel Masse.

Other details about the campaign that leaked out suggested that the "hardball players" Campbell had brought on board had done their work perhaps too well. Ross Howard of *The Globe and Mail* reported that the Campbell team used the fact that she was supported by sixteen ministers "seeking re-election compared to Mr. Charest's two" to strong-arm delegates into staying with Campbell. "When delegate polls indicated that Ms. Campbell could still win, some of her Quebec lieutenants turned up the pressure: to abandon her now is never to be forgiven, they warned."[30]

On the Tuesday following the convention, Mulroney introduced Campbell to a gathering of the whole caucus with a rousing call for absolute dedication to the new leader. But when Campbell made special mention of Charest in her speech, Charest sat stone-faced while his colleagues applauded him. He had already revealed that his place in the cabinet had not yet been determined. Rumours were circulating that Campbell had promised the biggest plum, the position of deputy prime minister to Perrin Beatty, the one-time leadership hopeful first to come over to Campbell's campaign.

The Charest camp was reportedly still furious over Campbell's treatment of their candidate in her acceptance speech. On her way to the mike after being introduced as the new prime minister, Campbell brushed by Charest and his wife with no gesture of recognition or friendship. Beyond referring to Charest as "one hell of a tortoise," Campbell made no reference to her need for him on her team. It was a reminder of what Campbell's old school board adversary, Phil Rankin, had said about her — that she was so egotistical that she was incapable of giving other people credit.

Although some within the party suggested that the animosity between the Campbell and Charest camps would soon die down — after all, they said, it was nothing compared to the old Clark-Mulroney tensions — others were not so sure. It was Clark's extraordinary willingness to forget the dirty tricks that the Mulroney people used against him that was key in resolving their dispute. Unless Campbell's trademark arrogance changed quickly, there was every prospect that Mulroney's legacy of a united Conservative Party would be lost. In the end, she was persuaded to extend the olive branch. She offered Charest the position of deputy prime minister.

Prime Minister Campbell

When Kim Campbell is asked just how she is different from Brian Mulroney, there is little satisfaction for those who want some assurance that the unpopular policies he pursued will be dropped. On March 25, the day she announced her candidacy, Campbell told reporters: "I think that there are all sorts of ways in which I am different from Brian Mulroney, by virtue of my generation, by virtue of where I come from, by virtue of my gender, by virtue of my own background. If I didn't think I had something new and fresh to offer I wouldn't be here."[1]

There is little of substance in her statement, certainly no hint of a different policy orientation. In fact, in matters of policy she is completely on side. "Well, I have no desire to distance myself from policies or priorities that I had a role in creating, whether they're unpopular or not."[2] And Campbell has suggested that the Mulroney government's policies are not as unpopular as polls indicate them to be.

When Campbell first announced her candidacy, Peter Mansbridge challenged her claim that she wanted to listen to people: "We see you standing here today saying that you stand foursquare behind the whole range of decisions which were massively unpopular: the GST, free trade, the helicopter deal, any number of things. And you say you have to defend those decisions. So, do you want to listen to people or don't you?"[3]

Campbell's response was that the polls suggesting she could win an election meant that the same policies could be sold with a different leader: "The assumption that Canadians hate everything the Conservatives have done is wrong."[4] With a different communications strategy, Campbell implied that she would succeed where Mulroney had failed in persuading Canadians they should support the Tory agenda.

It is important to understand that Campbell actually believes that public ignorance and a lack of effective communication were the source of the Mulroney government's problems. These statements are consistent with Campbell's political philosophy that an intellectual élite should guide the country.

This world view is crucial to understanding Campbell and how she sees politics and the record that she says she helped implement. Polls demonstrated consistently that a large majority of Canadians disagreed profoundly with virtually every aspect of the Tory agenda. The experience of the 1991–92 Spicer Commission in its cross-Canada hearings on the constitution was that people were demanding democratic reform to get "responsive and responsible political leadership," the kind of leadership they felt had been absent with Mulroney. Campbell, however, remains convinced that Canadian democracy is working exactly as it should, aside perhaps from a failure to communicate.

Promoting the Tory Agenda

Campbell willingly accepts full responsibility for the Tory policies implemented since the election of 1988. And so she should, because from February 1990 when she was appointed Justice Minister, Campbell sat on the most important committees of the Mulroney government, including the planning and priorities committee. This committee, made up of Mulroney's most senior and trusted cabinet members, decided every major policy initiative, how each policy would be sold to the public and which election promises would be dropped. More than any other role Campbell played, this one establishes that she was not merely along for the ride. She had her hands on the steering wheel as Mulroney kept the promise he made in 1984: "We have been in power for only two months, but I can tell you this: give us twenty years, and it is coming, and you will not recognize this country."[5] It has been only nine years, but many Canadians are already finding it difficult to recognize their country. It is worth reviewing the policies that the Conservatives have implemented since 1988 to determine where Campbell stands.

Free Trade

Signed in 1988, the free trade agreement was the centrepiece of the Conservative government's restructuring of Canada — of making it, as in Mulroney's promise, "unrecognizable." The restructuring has benefited almost exclusively only the largest Canadian and transnational corporations and the wealthiest Canadians.

When Campbell was campaigning in Vancouver Centre during the 1988 election, she screamed "What are you people so afraid of?" at anti–free trade hecklers.[6] Answering Campbell's question today appears depressingly easy. Virtually all of the warnings about the deal have come true: massive job losses; loss of control over energy resources to the United States; cuts to social programs and medicare as governments try to create a level playing field by lowering corporate tax rates; the prevention of any new social initiatives by the public sector, resulting in the failure of governments to implement new programs such as public auto insurance in Ontario.

In the three years preceding the deal, 1986 through 1988, 1,024,000 new jobs were created in Canada. In the three years following the implementation of the deal, 1989 through 1991, Canada experienced a net *decline* of 122,000 jobs.[7] While some of these job losses were temporary ones caused by the recession, 60 percent of the post-free trade losses have been permanent. By way of contrast, in the 1982 recession only 20 percent of the job losses were permanent.

Peter C. Newman has remarked on how distinctive this deal is in relation to the trade agreements of other developed nations: "The most immediate effect of free trade has been the accelerated de-industrialization of Canada; we've gone straight from smokestacks to warehouses ... Canada is establishing an unheard-of precedent. We are about to become the only country in recorded history to reverse the traditional evolution from underdevelopment to a manufacturing economy."[8]

Campbell aggressively supported the free trade agreement in Vancouver Centre and that support did not go unnoticed in Ottawa. Her enthusiasm for the deal and her ferocious attacks on its opponents caught Brian Mulroney's eye. Mulroney chose her to give the reply to the Speech from the Throne at the beginning of his second mandate, an honour for someone who had been a Conservative for only a few months and a sign that Mulroney was expecting big things from this rookie MP.

Campbell did not disappoint her boss. The reply to the Throne Speech focused on praise for the free trade deal. Claiming that it addressed British Columbia's historic grievances regarding tariffs,

Campbell stated that the deal had been sought by businesses "large and small" and that "the path to greater prosperity lies in removing the training wheels of protectionism." Distorting criticism of the deal as she did during the election, Campbell told the House: "The greatest threat to the survival of Canada as a nation is not trade with the U.S. ... [it] is the perception in the regions of Canada that the cost of confederation is too high. The free trade agreement does more for regional development than any policy in our history ... Mr Speaker I am proud to support the free trade agreement."[9]

Many Mulroney government policies have compounded the problems caused by free trade. The high dollar and the interest rates that keep it high have not only harmed exports but also created the worst unemployment rate since the Great Depression — nearly twice as high as the rate in the United States. These same high interest rates are responsible for nearly half of Canada's accumulated national debt and much of the provincial debt, as well.

Poverty and Unemployment

Levels of poverty in Canada reached the point where, at the end of May 1993, a United Nations committee gave Canada "what is believed to be the harshest attack it has ever launched concerning the performance of an industrialized nation."[10] Canada was criticized for its failure to address the problem of poverty, for allowing food banks and charities to substitute for government action, for a housing situation so bad that single mothers were being forced to give up their children because they could not afford to house them. Canada may be the only developed country to have eliminated all spending on social housing at the national level.

In one section of the report, the UN committee took aim at Canada's failure to see freedom from poverty as a human right — a comment that speaks directly to Campbell's hostility to rights and entitlement. It criticized the Charlottetown accord for listing social and economic rights under the category "social policy objectives" rather than as "fundamental human rights."[11]

On these issues — unemployment and poverty — Campbell and her cabinet colleagues have little to say. During her leadership campaign, Campbell rarely talked about unemployment and never mentioned the word *poverty* in dozens of statements, interviews and responses in her debates with other candidates. One of Camp-

bell's supporters in the Tory caucus, Barbara Greene, had plenty
to say about poverty, however. Greene, who chairs the Commons
subcommittee on poverty, led it in redefining its mandate to investigate not how to address the problem, but how to ratchet down
the definition of poverty in order to reduce the number of Canadians below the poverty line. This extraordinary mandate
prompted the opposition parties to boycott the committee.

Campbell will continue the implementation of the neo-conservative Tory agenda. There is nothing to suggest that she will not,
and in fact she made her intentions very clear throughout her
leadership campaign. She has stated on many occasions that she
continues to support fully the record of the Mulroney government
and was proud to be part of it. Her place on the planning and
priorities committee testifies to her active participation in design-
ing and carrying out that agenda. Testimony from her own cabinet
colleagues and journalists' observations suggest that she was one
of the most enthusiastic promoters of all the key policies of Mulroney's second term.

During the course of the leadership campaign, Campbell declared the principle of universality dead; questioned the viability
of the current medicare system by hinting to the provinces that she
might allow user fees; and questioned old age pensions. Her radical debt reduction plan, which she promised would be carried out
with no new taxes and no cuts to the military budget, placed her
to the right of Brian Mulroney. Mulroney intervened during the
course of the leadership campaign to warn candidates against
attacking universality in health care, as Campbell and Charest had
begun to do. A Campbell government will ensure massive cuts to
social spending and further transfers of wealth to those already
wealthy. Under Campbell, the implementation of the North
American Free Trade Agreement with Mexico and the United
States is a certainty. The rapid end to farm subsidies, marketing
boards and regional development assistance have not been promised. But they should be expected.

Campbell was on the priorities and planning committee when
it made successive decisions to slash the budget of the CBC. She
was there when the cabinet cut VIA Rail — and during her leadership campaign ridiculed those who were upset by the decision:
"You'd think we had engaged in the mass slaughter of the Canadian beaver." She was there when the cabinet cut the Environment Department's Green Plan by over one-third — effectively

killing it. One of Campbell's few references to the environment was a remark directed against environmentalists: "I've always been interested in going to visit people in my own province who are very hostile to forest development. They inevitably live in log houses and have wood-burning fireplaces."[12]

Campbell has committed herself publicly to the privatization of Air Canada; the expenditure of billions of dollars on the Hibernia oil megaproject; the GST and Tory tax reform, which made the taxes on Canada's wealthy the lowest in the industrialized world; the elimination of universality in family allowances; cuts to Unemployment Insurance; and cutting provincial transfer payments for health, education and social assistance.

Using the Debt to Cut Social Programs

In her response to an opposition motion critical of the government's cuts to regional development, agriculture and child care in the 1989 budget, Campbell took up the new Tory strategy for chipping away at social programs. The erosion of social programs would be linked to the national debt. It would be portrayed as unrelated to free trade. Cuts in taxes to wealthy Canadians and large corporations were justified by the need to create a "level playing field" with the United States and virtually guaranteed a continuing and convenient debt "crisis." Campbell presented the party's deficit-cutting policies as originating in a concern for future generations. In a long speech on the government's first post-election budget that focused almost exclusively on the debt, Campbell repeated one theme over and over again: "I do not want to have to face a young generation who will reproach me with the debt that I have incurred and put on their backs because I am not prepared to take the tough decisions to reduce the national debt."[13]

Reminding the House of the "social goals" the Tories allegedly shared with the opposition, Campbell stated: "What a tragedy if we do not have the money to support those social goals because our tax dollars are increasingly going to pay interest on the national debt."[14] While the implication was support for common social goals, Campbell also delivered up a bit of the "tough love" advocated by her previous boss, B.C. Premier Bill Bennett: "Unlike the New Democratic Party, our Government does not view Canadians as victims and does not see it as the role of government to perpetuate weakness and dependency."[15]

The Tories' own Task Force on Program Review, chaired in the mid-eighties by Erik Nielsen, demonstrated that Canada has been in a revenue crisis for almost fifteen years — not a debt crisis. A 1991 Statistics Canada Study[16] showed that 50 percent of Canada's debt was due to tax breaks and loopholes. High interest charges — another Tory policy — accounted for 44 percent of the debt. Just 6 percent of the debt was due to increased spending since 1975 — and just a third of that was spending on social programs.

Government members would have been familiar with the results of the Nielsen task force. The focus on reducing the debt through social program cuts was, according to Maude Barlow, "one of the most singularly dishonest campaigns ever waged by government in this country ... Every Tory M.P. and cabinet minister was conscripted into service of the 'new' crisis ... that the government had deceitfully neglected to address during the election."[17] Campbell had been given the honour of being one of the first conscripts.

Tory Democracy

Campbell fully supports the record of the government that she served for over four years, a record that includes not only particular policies but also particular ways of implementing these policies. The Mulroney government's history of negotiating behind closed doors, forcing through unpopular legislation by appointing its friends to the Senate and using fear tactics to promote free trade and constitutional reform created the conditions for a movement for democratic reform. Mulroney's actions gave the Reform Party, which in normal times would have been a regional protest party, the push it needed to become a national force on the basis of its promises of political reform. Mechanisms of direct democracy — recall of MPs, referenda — and other democratic reforms such as free votes in the Commons, which previously had generated little interest in Canada, now became popular as Canadians considered how prime ministers like Mulroney could be stopped in the future.

Despite Campbell's stated intention to "include the people" and to change the way politics are "done," she supported methods like closure that limit debate and inclusion. "The very week that Kim Campbell was coming out calling for more people involvement," recalls Betty Baxter, Campbell's NDP opponent in Vancouver

Centre in 1993, "she stood up in the House and voted against striking a committee to study the right to die — not against a law, just against having any public discussions about it; voted as part of the Tory caucus to limit the time allocation [for debate] on the unemployment insurance bill and then voted to pass it after one day's debate; and on the day she announced her candidacy when she was talking about more open consultation, the Tories voted to introduce time allocation [limiting debate] on NAFTA to two days — that's two days on what is arguably the most important legislation in two decades."[18]

Aside from a vague reference to allowing more freedom of expression for MPs in Parliament, Campbell indicated she thought the cure for the public's disaffection with government was not to change policies or methods of implementation, but to change the way the government communicated and to involve people so that they could better understand the government's position.

Campbell's attitude to human rights and entitlement and her characterization of advocacy groups as "interest groups" promise an erosion of democracy as Canadians have come to understand it. A devotee of the narrowest possible definition of parliamentary democracy, Campbell genuinely believes that rule by the élite, the "civically competent," serves the common good. Democratic practice, in this conception, is reduced to voting in elections. The only other way to participate legitimately in public life, the meaning of Campbell's offer of "inclusiveness," is to join a political party.

Manipulating Public Opinion

It would not have mattered how many people opposed the GST, the Mulroney government would not have reversed its course. Their chief pollster was Allan Gregg, the man who helped design the "Tough Guy" campaign for Bill Bennett. Allan Gregg, Norman Spector, Gerry Lampert and Patrick Kinsella were the political operators who boasted of their ability to manipulate public opinion during Bill Bennett's campaign in 1982–83. From Bennett, they moved on to Mulroney's team in 1983–84, and the use of political spin doctors and poll manipulators soon became the rule rather than the exception.

These are the men who have been credited with the first use in Canada of American-style political polling — the kind intended to massage voters out of their beliefs by first identifying their values and then persuading them that conservative policies actually reflected those values. They also pioneered the "big bang" approach to implementing policies — keep your electoral agenda secret and then act on all the harshest measures in your agenda at once in order to fragment opposition that will have to fight the government on a number of fronts.

The Tories sold free trade to the Canadian public, tried to sell the GST, and are now selling deficit reduction with what has become known as the TINA argument: There Is No Alternative. For governments intent on reversing decades of social policy in a short time, changing people's values just takes too long. It is easier to persuade people that their values, good as they are, are not practical, that they can no longer find their way into public policy.

Campbell has her own version of this theme: "There is no limit to the good we can do but there are limits to the good we can afford to do."[19] The TINA argument is the ideological companion to the big-bang strategy employed by Bennett in 1983. It amounts to creating a retroactive consensus, and it fits perfectly with Campbell's view of democracy as government by an élite.

Neo-conservatives network on an international scale and share strategies and experiences, so predictably a pattern emerges in the implementation of their agenda. The Conservative government of Grant Devine in Saskatchewan contracted the Fraser Institute and Margaret Thatcher's advisor, Madsen Pirie, to help them with their privatization plans; Milton Friedman admired and kept close tabs on the political effectiveness of Bennett's restraint program; Tory advisors work closely with their Republican counterparts in the United States and attend their political strategy schools.[20] Preston Manning invited New Zealand's neo-conservative guru Sir Roger Douglas as the keynote speaker to the Reform Party's 1991 convention. It was Douglas who most openly called for keeping the neo-conservative agenda secret, for retroactive consensus: "The conventional view is that consensus support must exist for reform before you start. ... [But] consensus for 'quality decisions' does not arise before they are made and implemented. It develops after they are taken."[21]

This approach to governing is supported by representatives of large corporations as well — in particular by the enormously influential Tom d'Aquino of the Business Council on National Issues. Responding to the charge that the imposition of the GST was a violation of democracy, d'Aquino bristled and referred to the experience of other countries that had imposed value-added taxes: "What we saw ... is that there would be strong resistance to reform and, after about eighteen months to three years, the new régime would be acceptable and people would get on with their lives."[22]

If Campbell is elected as prime minister in the next election, there is good reason to suspect a replay of the 1983 B.C. Social Credit campaign, the "Tough Guy for tough times" theme that beat NDP leader Dave Barrett. Campbell has already shown that she is preparing for just such a campaign. Her Draconian fiscal policy would necessitate a sudden round of reforms not unlike those instituted by the Bennett government. Kinsella and Lampert (and possibly Spector), who pioneered the "retroactive consensus" approach to democracy, will likely still be advising her. And Campbell has a proven track record of sticking to her policies regardless of the pressure from "interest groups," even if these groups represent a majority of Canadians.

Judging Campbell's Political Philosophy

Brian Mulroney began his political career on the moderate side of Tory politics. In his first leadership campaign in 1976, Mulroney tried to garner the support of Red Tories and other moderates because that is where his sentiments lay. But out of expediency, over the years Mulroney increasingly came to embrace neo-conservatism.

Campbell is different. Her politics derive a consistency of outlook from a very specific political philosophy — Edmund Burke's. This attraction is not just a passing fancy: Campbell repeatedly refers to Burke in her speeches, in her comments on policy in the House of Commons, in her interviews with journalists probing what makes her tick as a politician. Campbell does not want to construct a political world exactly as Burke would have, where only a limited number of people would be allowed to vote. But we must credit Campbell with adherence to a coherent political viewpoint. Burke believed that the concept of democracy should be limited in terms of the political role played by the ordinary citizen. The vast majority of people were, in Burke's view, "politically incapable ..." He warned that "God and nature never made them to think or act without guidance and direction."[23] Burke's views are echoed in Campbell's comments about the defeat of the Charlottetown accord in her speech at Harvard. It was the educated, those who understood Canada, who voted Yes and the "civically incompetent" who voted No.[24]

Burke did not believe that people's grievances should be ignored. "But for the real cause [of their distress] or the appropriate remedy, they ought never be called into council about one or the other." Good public policy for the benefit of the whole community must be determined "by those, who by their rank and fortune in the country, by the goodness of their characters, and their experience in their affairs, are their natural leaders."[25]

Those natural leaders, the "civically competent," in Campbell's phrase, are the élite. "In all societies, consisting of various descriptions of citizens, some descriptions must be uppermost," wrote Burke.[26] Political scientist Francis Canavan paraphrases Burke: "Civil society necessarily generates a 'natural aristocracy' of men who by native ability, education, wealth, and even inherited rank, are properly qualified to rule. Egalitarianism, which would deny the presumption in favour of rule by this class, is a crime, not so much against them as against society. The aristocracy is the bulwark of liberty, protecting society against ... popular tyranny."[27]

And what of unpopular or even wrong decisions by this élite? "The people," Burke said, "are presumed to consent to whatever the Legislature ordains for their benefit; and they are to acquiesce in it, though they do not clearly see into the propriety of the means, by which they are conducted to that desirable end. This they owe as an act of homage and just deference to reason, which the necessity of Government has made superior to their own."[28]

In Burke's philosophy, we find a great deal to explain Campbell's behaviour and attitude towards public opposition to Tory policies. For Campbell, resistance to the GST and free trade should be ignored as a "popular tyranny" by those who simply are not capable of understanding what is good for them. In pure Burkean fashion, she responded to public opposition to programs such as the helicopter purchase by saying that she would persist and do the "right" thing.

Campbell herself has said that the key to understanding her views is to know her underlying belief system. In her now-famous conversation with Peter C. Newman, Campbell said, "What I tried to impart to my students was how to go back and look at the fundamental premises of a belief system. If you and I argue about something ... we're starting from fundamentally different premises; you may construct very sound arguments but if we don't share the same premises we're probably not going to get to the same place."[29]

Campbell's premises about human nature make her an ideological conservative, and no matter how sound the arguments of those seeking policies based on egalitarian principles, she and they will not "get to the same place." When Campbell talks of "inclusion," she does not mean that she will include in her policy considerations the views of those with different belief systems. When she says she wants to talk to people, she does not mean that she is going to change her mind based on what they say. Rather, she wants to persuade them that she is right. She wants them to come over to her belief system. She wants them to become Conservatives.

Ironically, Campbell's ardent support for the Tory agenda involves promoting just the sort of "revolutionary" change that her philosophy preaches against. For over twenty years in Canada, egalitarian principles have been established as a fundamental sign of a civilized society. These principles have become part of the custom and political culture through a legitimate political process. Through the growth and acceptance of the idea of human rights and entitlement and through the formal involvement in the political process of women, aboriginals and other groups, the nature of democracy in Canada has changed. Part of why Canadians were so outraged at the imposition of the GST is that they had come to expect more of their democracy than the "stewardship" of an élite. They expected democracy to work between elections because they had been a part of the process that changed it in that egalitarian direction. In her promotion of the élite politics of "stewardship" — doing what is right, not what is popular — Campbell intends a conservative "revolution" that will turn back the clock.

Campbell's Feminism

Clearly, Campbell departs from her favourite philosopher regarding the role of women in society and in politics, because Edmund Burke was no feminist. Campbell is prepared to welcome social change as positive and rational where her immediate personal experience tells her that the "natural aristocracy of men" is an inadequate understanding of democracy. Campbell's feminism goes just as far as is necessary to include women in the "natural aristocracy," and no further. Her feminism is not, for the most part, in conflict with her élitist view of democracy.

Campbell has described herself as a feminist many times, typically in the way she explained it to Peter C. Newman. "I was raised to be a feminist but all feminists do not necessarily walk in ideological lockstep. What unites us is our passion for equality of women ... But the world as women see it is not going to be uniform: there are feminists who think that to be a feminist you have to be left wing."[30]

The equality of women Campbell speaks of is not equality *amongst* women. There is no sisterhood for Campbell, as one of her MP supporters, anti-abortionist Benno Friesen, hastens to point out. "She has one notion of feminism and that is equality. She told me that personally — she assumes women are equal. She is not on a crusade about women being equal."[31]

Feminists are not all in agreement about Campbell's claim to be one of them. Judy Rebick, the outspoken past president of the National Action Committee, sees Campbell as firmly on the far right of the political spectrum in social and economic policy. But she acknowledges that Campbell is a feminist — in a very limited sense and on a narrow range of issues. "Her vision of getting women into positions of power is so limited. She supports economic and social policies that will marginalize women and keep women poor, so it's basically women who are already in an advantaged position whom she is going to help get into positions of power."[32]

Campbell has said that women's experience has to inform public policy. On this issue, Rebick gives Campbell credit for the rape shield law, but says: "With [that exception] she hasn't come through on a single question."[33] Human rights activist and NAC executive member Shelagh Day speaks sharply and to the point: "By their deeds shall you know them. It's not enough for a politician to say she's a feminist. Politicians say a lot of things. I want to see what they fight for, what they stand up for, what they actually do. By this standard I have some real questions about Kim Campbell."[34]

Campbell's élite-biased feminism is revealed in a number of her comments. Rebick recalls Campbell's response to the B.C. government's proposal for gender equity in the Senate: "She said, 'What NAC should do is look at the conflict of interest laws. They affect women disproportionately because their [male] spouses are more likely to be in a conflict situation.' This was her main recommendation for removing the barriers to women in politics. What she's concerned about are women whose husbands are rich and are therefore barriers to them running. She can't see the world from any other perspective."[35]

Yet there are women who are attracted to Campbell almost despite themselves — in part because of who attacks Campbell and from what point on the political spectrum. REAL Women and anti-abortion groups targeted Campbell in the leadership campaign as being a "radical feminist," and "pro-homosexual." Gwen Landolt, vice-president of REAL Women, told *The Globe and Mail*'s Miro Cernetig that "they had been plotting since Christmas to stop Ms. Campbell. Landolt described Campbell as a "Red Tory."[36] Writer Susan Riley saw REAL Women's attacks on Campbell "as good enough a reason as any, to support her."[37]

Other women are attracted to Campbell because, in Rebick's view, "She has what a lot of other female Tories do not have ... She's saying [to women] 'I'm a woman, I'm powerful, and I am not going to be like a man to be powerful.' And that's very appealing to women because for so long women thought that they had to be like men to succeed — like Margaret Thatcher. She really does speak to a lot of professional women."[38]

But in the final analysis, says Rebick, "Campbell will be able to much more effectively marginalize the women's movement than Mulroney ever could — by claiming that she represents women and that we [feminists] are a radical, marginal fringe. Thatcherism destroyed the women's movement in Britain, and Campbell could repeat that here."[39]

"Judgement, Judgement, Judgement"

In her talk with Peter C. Newman, Campbell offered the following opinion: "I guess in my view the three things that are most important in a politician are judgement, judgement, judgement."[40] In retrospect, this statement might be hazardous for Campbell because in the eyes of many observers it is precisely in the area of judgement that Campbell is so often found wanting.

It was during her leadership campaign that the question of judgement came up most often and most dramatically. Observers and supporters alike were dumbfounded by what seemed to be terrible lapses in judgement. The "enemies of Canadians" comment cost her dearly; her "demons of the papacy" was taken out of context, but as an experienced politician she should have realized that it would be; and calling Canadians who are not involved in a political party "condescending SOB's" went beyond "candour" — many found it offensive. These are not comments Campbell made when she was out of the limelight and could hope they would be ignored. Campbell expressed these views during the time she was either organizing her campaign behind the scenes or actually in the heat of the campaign.

Perhaps the most revealing comment Campbell made was when she suggested that it was not illegal to smoke marijuana. She could have written off her experimenting with marijuana as an error of youth, but she could not bring herself to say she had made a mistake. Asked by Newman if she could identify any flaws in her character, the only thing she could think of was that she did not like talking on the telephone. But Campbell's inability to resist always proving herself smarter than others could be described as a fundamental flaw in her character that affects her judgement.

It is this constant need to prove herself that gives the impression that Campbell is constantly applying for a job. She has retained the habit of exaggerating her accomplishments and her qualifications from the beginning of her career. She refers to herself as an intellectual but, as an academic, she does not have a single published paper or article to her credit. There is no indication she has done any original research or thinking, and she dropped out of both the master's and the doctoral programs she began.

Campbell claims to have taken strategic studies when in fact she studied Soviet politics. She allows exaggerated claims to slip by uncorrected, notably the ones about the number of languages she speaks. She refers repeatedly to her experience as a lawyer and dismisses women opposition MPs who do not have a legal background as unqualified to express their view of the law; however, her actual experience working in a law office lasted for a grand total of sixteen months — twelve of those as an apprentice articling student. She claims to have small-business experience yet has never actively run a business. She simply owned shares in a restaurant.

What is odd about all this is that people from across the political spectrum will grant that Campbell is very bright and does have genuine intellectual ability. There is no need for her to promote herself constantly in the way that she does. Rather than increase her stature in people's eyes, she does the opposite, raising questions about her judgement because the exaggerations she engages in are the kind that are, and have been, easily exposed.

In the House of Commons, answering questions, making statements, defending policies, Campbell has shown good judgement and real competence. She handles herself better than most cabinet ministers. And her judgement in getting controversial bills through the caucus and cabinet has been praised — at least by Mulroney and her other colleagues, if not by those who perceived her as compromising her principles. Campbell's ability to make apparently sound judgements in other areas of her political life make her obvious gaffes and petty exaggerations that much more puzzling.

Campbell's Political Debts

In assessing Campbell's fitness to be prime minister, it is fair to ask to whom she owes political debts. All politicians who have risen to the highest position in a political party have political debts to pay. The size and the implications of these debts are magnified a hundredfold if that person is also prime minister. The freedom of action of a prime minister is determined partly by the balance of credits and debits. In other words, a leader who has debts to call in as well as debts to pay is able to maintain some independence from the demand for patronage and favours.

A neophyte in Conservative Party insider politics, Campbell has few credits to call in and many, many debts to pay. Campbell came into the party from Social Credit in late 1988. Almost from the beginning of her time as an MP, she was burdened with the onerous duties of a cabinet position. She had little time for party work, even in her own constituency, which she left in the hands of staff and a constituency executive. In short, Campbell had little base to begin with and had no time to build one once she joined Mulroney's cabinet.

Campbell's rapid rise to prominence in the Mulroney government was in some ways a real disadvantage for her leadership aspirations. Winning the leadership of a national party in Canada entails having a large and effective network within that party — a network that usually combines a base of genuine grassroots support and professional political operatives who can find the money and make a campaign work. Again, it is a question of balance — the more solid the grassroots support, the less dependent a candidate is on political operatives.

Campbell's peculiar situation — as an outsider with virtually no political debts to call in — means that she will inevitably be beholden to those who engineered her victory in the leadership campaign. In this situation she contrasts sharply with both Brian Mulroney and Joe Clark, the two previous Tory leaders who laboured for years for the party before running for office. They had their friends and admirers across the country. They were known quantities, they could make personal phone calls to key people when they needed help, they had paid their dues by helping out on the campaigns of people who now supported them, and they had their own information networks.

Campbell went into the leadership campaign almost totally dependent on others. With no base in the grass roots and few key people with whom she had developed relationships over the years, with only a brief apprenticeship in how the party worked — and not many real friends in the party — Campbell was the establishment candidate in the worst possible sense. They virtually owned her. This was demonstrated most dramatically in the backroom start-up of her campaign. It was not initiated by Campbell because she could not initiate it; she could not make the first phone call because there was no one she could call. That "first call" was made by Brian Mulroney when he asked Marcel Masse to start the ball rolling.

That was the first debt, and the faster things moved, the more debts she acquired. The more her "winability factor" improved, the more old-time party hacks and public relations firms came on board and the more debts she accumulated. There is no question about what these debts actually entail. The high-rollers around Campbell expect to be rewarded — their livelihood depends on it. When these men do not get their rewards, they can be very nasty indeed, as Joe Clark discovered. Mulroney made no such mistake. And Campbell, the "quick study" in politics, will not be in a position to do anything different. Her list of people waiting for rewards will be longer and those on it more demanding for the very reason that they know, as she does, that she owes it all to them. One of those she owes the most to is Paul Curley, the man who already "holds more IOUs than a finance company." Campbell's new way of doing politics will be, of necessity, very much like the old way, if she wants to survive as Tory leader.

Notes

CHAPTER 1
1. Judy Steed, "In pursuit of power," *The Toronto Star*, 1 May 1993.
2. Steed.
3. Steed.
4. Steed.
5. Steed.
6. E. Kaye Fulton and Mary Janigan, "The Real Kim Campbell," *Maclean's*, 17 May 1993.
7. Fulton and Janigan.
8. Peter C. Newman, "Citizen Kim," *Vancouver Magazine*, May 1993.
9. Steed.
10. Fulton and Janigan.
11. Steed.
12. Charlotte Gray, *Saturday Night, October 1991*.
13. Newman.
14. Stan Persky, *Maclean's*, 17 May 1993.
15. Steed.
16. Leo Panitch, interview with the author.
17. Newman.
18. Charlotte Gray, *Chatelaine*, September 1990.
19. Newman.
20. Phil Rankin, interview with the author.
21. Susan Davis, interview with the author.
22. Kitty O'Callaghan, interview with the author.
23. Rankin.
24. Fulton and Janigan.
25. Ken Denike, interview with the author.
26. O'Callaghan.
27. Denike.
28. Davis.
29. Denike.
30. Rankin.
31. Rankin.
32. Fulton and Janigan.
33. Denike.
34. Fulton and Janigan.
35. Rankin.
36. Allan Garr, *Tough Guy: Bill Bennett and the Taking of British Columbia* (Toronto: Key Porter Books, 1985).
37. Garr, 91, 93.
38. Garr, 40.
39. Garr, 42.
40. Garr, 46.
41. Garr, 48-50.
42. Garr, 50.
43. Garr, 46.
44. Gary Lauk, interview with the author.
45. Lauk.
46. Lauk.
47. Garr.
48. Garr, 2.
49. Garr, 112.
50. Garr, 94.
51. Bryan Palmer, *Solidarity, The Rise and Fall of an Opposition in British Columbia* (Vancouver: New Star Books, 1987), 10.
52. Denike.
53. *CitySchools* magazine, a publication of the Vancouver school board, March 1983.
54. Davis.
55. Carol Volkart, "Kim Campbell: She's got the world by a string," Vancouver *Sun*, 29 January 1983.
56. Davis.
57. Denike.
58. Garr, 147.
59. Davis.
60. Denike.
61. Lauk.
62. Bud Smith, personal interview with the author.
63. Garr, 95.
64. Charlotte Gray, *Saturday Night*.
65. Steed.
66. Rankin.
67. Newman.
68. Gillian Shaw, "Campbell: Intellectual lawyer sees her politics as chance to enlighten," Vancouver *Sun*, 3 July 1986.
69. Darlene Marzari, interview with the author.
70. Marzari.
71. Vancouver *Sun*, 3 July 1986.
72. Steed.
73. Philip Resnick, interview with the author.
74. Keith Baldry, Vancouver *Sun*, 11 March 1988.
75. Baldry.
76. Steed.

CHAPTER 2
1. Charlotte Gray, "Justice Minister

Kim Campbell," *Chatelaine,*
September 1990.
2. Tim Harper, *The Toronto Star,* 28
November 1988.
3. Gary Mason, Vancouver *Sun,*
12 October 1988.
4. Tex Enemark, personal interview with
the author.
5. Thomas Walkom, *The Globe and Mail,*
25 October 1988.
6. Gray, "Justice Minister."
7. Mark Hume, Vancouver *Sun,* 19
October 1988.
8. Hume.
9. Hume.
10. Victoria *Times Colonist,* 19
November 1988.
11. Enemark.
12. Charlotte Gray, *Saturday Night,*
October 1991.
13. Gray, "Justice Minister."
14. *Times Colonist.*
15. *Times Colonist.*
16. Hume.
17. Enemark.
18. Hume.
19. Les Leyne, Victoria *Times Colonist,*
19 November 1988.
20. Iain Hunter, Ottawa *Citizen,* 10
November 1988.
21. Hunter.
22. Walkom.
23. Lauro de Hann, personal interview
with the author.
24. *The Globe and Mail,* 8 April 1993.
25. Saskatoon *Star-Phoenix,* 29 March
1993.
26. Janet McPhee and Cherie Miltimore,
personal interviews with the author.
27. McPhee and Miltimore.
28. "Solemn Declaration," Costa Penn,
affidavit signed before a
commissioner of oaths, 3 December
1992.
29. Letter from Jonathon Baker to
Granville Island Parents Association,
2 December 1992.
30. McPhee and Miltimore.
31. McPhee and Miltimore.
32. McPhee and Miltimore.
33. McPhee and Miltimore.
34. McPhee and Miltimore.
35. McPhee and Miltimore.
36. McPhee and Miltimore.
37. McPhee and Miltimore.
38. These figures were provided by The
Granville Island Parents Association.

39. Lauro de Haan, personal interview
with the author.
40. De Haan.
41. De Haan.
42. De Haan.
43. De Haan.
44. De Haan.
45. De Haan.
46. E. Kaye Fulton and Mary Janigan,
"The Real Kim Campbell,"
Maclean's, 17 May 1993.
47. Enemark.
48. *The Globe and Mail,* 24 November
1988.
49. Fulton and Janigan.
50. Enemark.
51. Enemark.
52. Enemark.
53. Enemark.
54. Betty Baxter, personal interview with
the author.
55. CBC "Prime Time News,"
24 March 1993.

CHAPTER 3
1. Stephen Bindman, "Equal Justice for
Women," Montreal *Gazette,* 15 June
1991.
2. Bindman.
3. Bindman.
4. Bindman.
5. Charlotte Gray, *Saturday Night,*
October 1991.
6. *The Globe and Mail,* 11 June 1991.
7. Gray.
8. Vancouver *Sun,* 11 June 1991.
9. Gray.
10. Gray.
11. Bindman.
12. Gray.
13. Gray.
14. Kim Campbell, "Judicial Review and
the Role of the Courts: Challenges in
Defining a Post-Charter Political
Culture," Ottawa, 14 April 1992.
Emphasis added.
15. Campbell.
16. Campbell.
17. Ken Norman, personal interview, 12
April 1993.
18. Norman.
19. Norman.
20. Norman.
21. Kim Campbell, "Unedited transcript
of the remarks made by the
Honourable A. Kim Campbell at the
Canada Seminar," Harvard
University, 10 November 1992.

22. Norman.
23. Norman.
24. Norman.
25. Campbell, "Unedited transcript."
26. Norman.
27. Kathleen Ruff, personal interview, March 1993.
28. Ruff, personal interview.
29. Norman.
30. Ruff, personal interview.
31. Norman.
32. Ruff, personal interview.
33. Norman.
34. Norman.
35. Norman.
36. Ruff, personal interview.
37. Shelagh Day.
38. Kathleen Ruff, "Final Appeal ," *Canadian Forum,* June 1992.
39. Pat File, personal interview.
40. Don Mazankowski, "To Anita Bhatia, Minority Advocacy and Rights Council," 21 August 1992.
41. *The Globe and Mail,* 1 May 1993.
42. Day, Williams and Thobani, "Scrap Canadian Human Rights Amendments!" Vancouver, 8 February 1993.
43. Day, Williams and Thobani.
44. Day, Williams and Thobani.
45. Day, Williams and Thobani.
46. Ruff, personal interview.
47. Ruff, personal interview.
48. Norman.

CHAPTER 4
1. Graham Fraser, "The Woman Behind the Robe," *The Globe and Mail,* 12 December 1992.
2. Charlotte Gray, *Saturday Night,* October 1991.
3. Charlotte Gray, "Justice Minister Kim Campbell," *Chatelaine,* September 1990.
4. Fraser.
5. Fraser.
6. Fraser.
7. Judy Steed, "In Pursuit of Power," *The Toronto Star,* 1 May 1993.
8. Angus Reid poll quoted in Coalition for Gun Control literature.
9. Wendy Cukier, interview with the author.
10. Cukier.
11. Heidi Rathjen, interview with the author.
12. List of organizational members, dated 8 March 1993.

13. Cukier.
14. Cukier.
15. Cukier.
16. Cukier.
17. Cukier.
18. Rathjen.
19. Cukier.
20. Rathjen.
21. Rathjen.
22. Cukier.
23. *The Toronto Star,* 1 March 1990.
24. Minutes of Parliamentary Committee Hearings into Bill C-43, 29 March 1990.
25. Shelagh Day, interview with the author.
26. Minutes of Parliamentary Com mittee Hearings.
27. Various correspondence from NAWL to several senators, 1990-91.
28. House of Commons, *Debates (Hansard),* 11 May 1990.
29. Letter from Kit Holmwood, CARAL, to Kim Campbell, 7 August 1990.
30. *The Toronto Star,* 29 September 1990.
31. *The Toronto Star,* 12 September 1990.
32. *Cambridge Times,* 8 November 1989.
33. Letter from CARAL to Senator Mabel DeWare, 17 January 1991.
34. Quoted in letter from CARAL to Senator Paul David, 23 January 1991.
35. *The Toronto Star,* 20 January 1991.
36. Leslie Pearl, NAWL, quoted in *The Globe and Mail,* 7 May 1990.
37. Senate Hearings, 29 October 1990.
38. Judy Rebick, interview with the author.
39. Rebick.
40. Rebick.
41. Rebick.
42. Rebick.
43. Rebick.
44. Rebick.
45. *The Globe and Mail,* 31 March 1993.
46. *The Globe and Mail,* 31 March 1993.
47. Charlotte Gray, *Saturday Night,* October 1991.
48. Day.
49. Day.
50. Day.

51. Rebick.
52. Rebick.
53. Gray, *Saturday Night.*
54. Peter Russell, interview with the author.
55. Russell.
56. Rebick.
57. Day.
58. *The Globe and Mail,* 12 December 1992.
59. *The Globe and Mail,* 12 December 1992.
60. *The Globe and Mail,* 12 December 1992.
61. House of Commons, *Debates (Hansard),* 1 April 1993.
62. Westray Mine Public Inquiry, Statement of John Merrick, QC, 30 March 1993.
63. Letter from Justice K. Peter Richard to Mr Dingwall, 5 August 1992.
64. Phil Rankin, interview with the author.

CHAPTER 5
1. *The Toronto Star,* 20 April 1992.
2. *The Globe and Mail,* 10 June 1992.
3. *The Toronto Star,* 20 April 1992.
4. *The Toronto Sun,* 12 June 1992.
5. *The Toronto Star,* 29 April 1992.
6. *The RHA Newsletter,* 25 March 1993.
7. CBC "Prime Time News" [special on the EH101], 27 April 1993.
8. *The Toronto Star,* 27 April 1993.
9. CBC "Prime Time News," 27 April 1993.
10. Statistics Canada, *Juristat Service Bulletin,* Vol. 1, no. 6, April 1990.
11. Statistics Canada, *Juristat Service Bulletin.*
12. *Wings,* 1988/1989: 119.
13. *Wings,* 1987/1988: 104.
14. Auditor General's Report, "Department of National Defence-Major Capital Projects Industrial Development Initiatives," November 1992.
15. *The Globe and Mail,* 6 May 1993.
16. Bill Robinson, Project Ploughshares.
17. *The Globe and Mail,* 11 March 1993.
18. The Saskatoon *Star-Phoenix,* 20 March 1993.
19. *The Toronto Star,* 27 April 1993.
20. John Sawatsky, *The Insiders,* 298.
21. Sawatsky, *The Insiders,* 299.
22. *The Globe and Mail,* 26 June 1992.
23. Ottawa *Citizen,* 22 October 1992.
24. Ottawa *Citizen,* 22 October 1992.
25. Advance Planning and Communications Inc., "A Communications Plan: NSA/NSH Program," June 1992.
26. Advance Planning and Communications Inc.
27. Rod McQueen, cited in John Sawatsky, *The Insiders,* 298.
28. John Sawatsky, *Mulroney: The Politics of Ambition,* 502.
29. Sawatsky, *The Insiders,* 282.
30. *The Globe and Mail,* 8 September 1992.
31. *The Globe and Mail,* 25 July 1993.
32. CBC "Prime Time News" [special report on the EH101], 27 April 1993.
33. *The Globe and Mail,* 25 July 1992.
34. CBC "Newsworld" [The Toronto Conservative Leadership Debate], 13 May 1993.
35. Ross Howard, *The Globe and Mail,* 6 May 1993.
36. Paul Koring, "Army pushed to breaking point," *The Globe and Mail,* 27 May 1993.
37. Halifax *Chronicle-Herald,* 16 February 1993.
38. Halifax *Chronicle-Herald,* 16 February 1993.
39. Montreal *Gazette,* 28 April 1993.
40. *The Toronto Star,* 29 April 1993.
41. *The Toronto Star,* 29 April 1993.
42. *The Globe* and *Mail,* 27 April 1993.
43. *The Globe and Mail,* 27 April 1993.
44. Geoffrey York, *The Globe and Mail,* 12 May 1993.
45. Geoffrey York, *The Globe and Mail,* 12 May 1993.
46. Geoffrey York, *The Globe and Mail,* 28 April 1993.

CHAPTER 6
1. *Globe and Mail*/ComQuest poll, March 1993.
2. Angus Reid poll, March 1993.
3. Gallup poll, March 1993.
4. Hugh Winsor and Ross Howard, "Potential candidates beat hasty retreat," *The Globe and Mail,* 16 March 1993.
5. CBC Radio, "Sunday Morning," 28 March 1993.
6. CBC "Prime Time News," 25 March 1993.
7. CBC "Prime Time News," 25 March 1993.
8. CBC "Prime Time News" interview, 25 March 1993.
9. *The Globe and Mail,* 26 March 1993.

10. *The Globe and Mail,* 4 March 1993.
11. *The Globe and Mail,* 4 March 1993.
12. Jason Moscovitz, CBC Radio, 26 March 1993.
13. John Sawatsky, *Mulroney: The Politics of Ambition,* 386.
14. Sawatsky, 387.
15. Sawatsky, 395.
16. *The Globe and Mail,* 12 March 1993, 19 March 1993.
17. Clare Hoy, *Friends in High Places,* (Toronto: Key Porter Books, 1987), 213.
18. Hoy, 354.
19. Graham Fraser, *The Globe and Mail,* 16 March 1993.
20. As told to Frances Russell, *Winnipeg Free Press.*
21. Richard Mackie, "Campbell charms, but speech falls flat," *The Globe and Mail,* 15 March 1993.
22. *The Globe and Mail,* 19 March 1993.
23. *The Globe and Mail,* 8 April 1993.
24. Hugh Winsor, "Wilson backs Segal in Tory race," *The Globe and Mail,* 7 April 1993.
25. *The Globe and Mail,* 8 April 1993.
26. *The Globe and Mail,* 17 April 1993.
27. *The Globe and Mail,* 17 April 1993.
28. CBC "Newsworld" [The Montreal Conservative Leadership Debate], 21 April 1993.
29. CBC "Newsworld" [The Montreal Conservative Leadership Debate], 21 April 1993.
30. Hugh Winsor, *The Globe and Mail,* 23 April 1993.
31. CBC "Newsworld" [The Montreal Conservative Leadership Debate], 21 April 1993.
32. CBC "Newsworld" [The Montreal Conservative Leadership Debate], 21 April 1993.
33. Ross Howard, "Campbell firm on helicopter purchase," *The Globe and Mail,* 6 May 1993.
34. *The Globe and Mail,* 30 April 1993.
35. *The Globe and Mail,* 30 April 1993.
36. Saskatoon *Star-Phoenix,* 6 April 1993.
37. Saskatoon *Star-Phoenix,* 6 April 1993.
38. *The Globe and Mail,* 30 April 1993.
39. *The Globe and Mail,* 30 April 1993.
40. *The Globe and Mail,* 8 April 1993.
41. *The Globe and Mail,* 20 April 1993.
42. *The Globe and Mail,* 8 April 1993.
43. *The Toronto Star,* 1 May 1993.
44. Kim Campbell, "Unedited transcript of the remarks made by the Honourable A. Kim Campbell at the Canada Seminar," Harvard University, 10 November 1992.

CHAPTER 7
1. Hugh Winsor, "Numbers favour a Campbell win," *The Globe and Mail,* 8 May 1993.
2. Susan Delacourt, "Gloves are off in Tory race," *The Globe and Mail,* 3 May 1993.
3. CBC "Prime Time News," 14 May 1993.
4. CBC "Prime Time News," 13 May 1993.
5. Peter C. Newman, "Citizen Kim," *Vancouver* Magazine, May 1993.
6. Newman.
7. Newman.
8. Newman.
9. Rhéal Séguin and Ross Howard, "Law not violated, Campbell believes," *The Globe and Mail,* 22 May 1993.
10. "Bill targets those seeking illicit drugs," Canadian Press, 1 June 1993.
11. Global News interview, 28 May 1993.
12. "No need to apologize: Campbell," *The Toronto Star,* 18 May 1993.
13. Hugh Winsor, "Media can't deal with candour, Campbell says," *The Globe and Mail,* 26 May 1993.
14. Winsor.
15. Winsor.
16. Newman.
17. "Poll results can sway 60% of delegates," *Financial Post,* 2 June 1993.
18. CBC News, convention special, 12 June 1993.
19. Radio Canada, special convention coverage, 13 June 1993.
20. CBC News, convention special, 13 June 1993.
21. Radio Canada, special convention coverage, 13 June 1993.
22. Radio Canada, special convention coverage, 13 June 1993.
23. CBC News, convention special, 13 June 1993.
24. CBC "Prime Time News," 10 June 1993.
25. CBC "Prime Time News," 10 June 1993.

26. Radio Canada, "Le Point," 10 June 1993.
27. Radio Canada, "Le Point," 10 June 1993.
28. CBC News, special convention coverage, 13 June 1993.
29. Hugh Winsor, "Charest supporters angry at Campbell," *The Globe and Mail,* 15 June 1993.
30. Ross Howard, "How Campbell's crew pulled out all the stops," *The Globe and Mail,* 15 June 1993.

CHAPTER 8
1. Transcript, Kim Campbell news conference, 25 March 1993.
2. Transcript, Kim Campbell news conference, 25 March 1993.
3. Transcript, CBC "Prime Time News," 25 March 1993.
4. Transcript, CBC "Prime Time News," 25 March 1993.
5. House of Commons, *Debates (Hansard),* 7 November 1984.
6. Victoria *Times Colonist,* 19 November 1988.
7. Mel Hurtig, *The Betrayal of Canada,* (1992), 22.
8. Peter C. Newman, *Maclean's,* 23 October 1989.
9. House of Commons, *Debates (Hansard),* 12 December 1988, 15, 16.
10. Geoffrey York, *The Globe and Mail,* 29 May 1993.
11. Geoffrey York, *The Globe and Mail,* 29 May 1993.
12. *The Globe and Mail,* 19 March 1993.
13. House of Commons, *Debates (Hansard),* 9 May 1989, 1472.
14. House of Commons, *Debates (Hansard),* 9 May 1989, 1472.
15. House of Commons, *Debates (Hansard),* 9 May 1989, 1470.
16. The study quoted was the original version of one written by H. Mimoto and P. Cross, released through the use of the Access to Information Act. As a result of intervention by the Finance Department, it was never published. The revised version was published in the June 1991 edition of *The Canadian Economic Observer,* under the title "The Growth of the Federal Debt." The original is available from the author.
17. Maude Barlow, *A Parcel of Rogues* (Toronto: Key Porter, 1990), 30.

18. Betty Baxter, personal interview, April 1993.
19. Shelagh Day, personal interview, reporting on human rights activists' meeting with Campbell, 27 February 1993.
20. Allan Garr, *Tough Guy: Bill Bennett and the Taking of British Columbia* (Toronto: Key Porter, 1985), 40.
21. Murray Dobbin, *Preston Manning and the Reform Party* (Halifax: Goodread, 1992), 135.
22. Murray Dobbin, "Taxes: The Second Certainty," CBC "Ideas," 23 April 1992.
23. Cited in Leo Strauss and Joseph Cropsey, *History of Political Philosophy,* (Rand McNally, 1969), 613.
24. Transcript of Campbell's address to the Canada Seminar, Harvard University, 20 November 1992. Campbell stated that the majority of Canadians are not "civically competent" to determine the course of the country.
25. Strauss and Cropsey, 612.
26. Strauss and Cropsey, 608.
27. Strauss and Cropsey, 608.
28. Strauss and Cropsey, 614.
29. Peter C. Newman, "Introducing Kim Campbell....," *The RHA Newsletter,* 25 March 1993: 11.
30. Newman.
31. Geoffrey York, "Why Campbell is not a Red Tory," *The Globe and Mail,* 31 March 1993.
32. Judy Rebick, interview with the author.
33. Geoffrey York, "Why Campbell is not a Red Tory."
34. Shelagh Day, interview with the author.
35. Rebick.
36. Miro Cernetig, "Campaign planned to stop Campbell on leadership trail," *The Globe and Mail,* 9 March 1993.
37. Susan Riley, "Ms. Representing Feminism: The Troubling Ascent of Kim Campbell," *This Magazine,* May 1983.
38. Rebick.
39. Rebick.
40. Newman.

Index